U 228
RAN

THE BOOK OF REVELATION:

What Does It Really Say?
by Rev. John Randall S.T.D.

THE BOOK OF REVELATION:
What Does It Really Say?

by Rev. John Randall S.T.D.

LIVING FLAME PRESS
BOX 74 LOCUST VALLEY, N.Y. 11560

All quotations of scripture are from **The New American Bible.**

Cover: Robert Manning

Published by: Living Flame Press/Locust Valley, N.Y. 11560

Copyright 1976: John Randall S.T.D.

ISBN: 0-914544-16-0

Printed in the United States of America

FOREWORD

"In view of the flood of statistics and the difficulties encountered by those who wish to plunge into historical narratives where the material is abundant, we have aimed to please those who prefer simple reading, as well as to make it easy for the studious who wish to commit things to memory, and to be helpful to all. For us who have taken upon ourselves the labor of making this digest, the task, far from easy, is one of sweat and sleepless nights, just as the preparation of a festive banquet is no light matter for one who thus seeks to give enjoyment to others. Similarly, to win the gratitude of many we will gladly endure these inconveniences, while we leave the responsibility for exact details to the original author, and confine our efforts to giving only a summary outline. As the architect of a new house must give his attention to the whole structure, while the man who undertakes the decoration and the frescoes has only to concern himself with what is needed for ornamentation, so I think it is with us. To enter into questions and examine them thoroughly from all sides is the task of the professional historian (exegete); but the man who is making an adaptation should be allowed to aim at brevity of expression and to omit detailed treatment of the matter. Here, then, we shall begin our account without further ado; it would be nonsense to write a long preface to a story and then abbreviate the story itself."
(2 Macchabees 2:24-32)

This passage articulates the type of work here envisaged. I do not wish to give the impression, however, that scholarly biblical homework is not involved. There are already too many unscholarly books on the market for me to add another. In fact, it was to shed some light on the present darkness that this work was attempted. The charismatic renewal particularly is deprived of much of its potential for renewing the Church by the current preponderance of fundamentalist exegesis. This is mainly true concerning the Book of Revelation.

Accordingly I wish to pay tribute to all biblical scholars, especially my fellow members of the Catholic Biblical Association to whom I owe so great a personal debt. Their painstaking effort to arrive at the original meaning of God's holy Word deserves the thanks and prayerful support of all who seek to live by that Word. It is to these devoted men and women that I wish to dedicate this little book.

I would also like to thank all who encouraged the publication of it, especially leaders of the Catholic Charismatic Renewal in the East where these talks were first given, and the book-tape ministry of St. Patrick's parish in Providence.

Finally, I wish to thank Sister Althea Margeson, R.S.M. and Mrs. Rose McLure who helped type the manuscript.

Rev. John Randall
Providence, R. I.

CONTENTS

Foreword 7

Introduction 11

Part One BIBLICAL BACKGROUND TO THE BOOK
OF REVELATION 15
  1. Matthew 24 and the Fall of Jerusalem 17
  2. Isaiah 13 and the Fall of Babylon 22
  3. The Book of Judith 25
  4. The Book of Daniel 27
  5. Characteristics of Apocalyptic Literature ... 30
  6. The "Apocalyptic Arsenal" 33
  7. Conclusion 37

Part Two THE BOOK OF REVELATION 41
  1. Chapter One, the Setting 43
  2. The Seven Letters to the Churches 48
  3. Chapter Four, The Heavenly Scene 53
  4. The Lamb and the Scroll 57
  5. The Seven Seals 60
  6. The Woman and the Dragon 74
  7. The Two Beasts 77
  8. "Babylon is Fallen" 81
  9. Victory of the Lamb 85

INTRODUCTION

St. Jerome, a fourth century scholar recognized as the patron of biblical scholarship, so loved God's word that he wanted to make its full meaning available to the people of his time. Accordingly, he undertook to study the original languages of the Bible and went to live in the Holy Land. He studied literary forms in biblical countries so that he could really get at the root of what God was saying to His people. He studied the times and contexts in which the work was originally spoken.

This quest shed much light, a light that has helped in understanding the Bible through the centuries. It has prompted great men like Augustine, Thomas Aquinas, Father LaGrange, and other scholars to spend their lives, in turn arriving at the essence of God's message to men. In this same tradition, we approach the very timely Book of Revelation.

There's a warning at the end of the book, originally found in Deuteronomy 4, that threatens woe to anyone who adds or subtracts from the word given by the Lord. This is a warning that has a lot of relevance today because, in my opinion, many are adding to what the author of Revelation originally wrote. They are doing this because they don't understand the historical context and, consequently, the original meaning of the book. We must come to understand what the original meaning of any book is before we can understand its application, its meaning for us today.

A few years ago, when the *New American Bible* first appeared, the introduction to the Book of Revelation began: "The Book of Revelation, or the Apocalypse, is the last book of the Bible and perhaps the least read." Today, that statement is no longer true. Something has happened and now Revelation is perhaps more read than any other book of the Bible. Why is that? I think it's because we live in a time of crisis. It has been said that we are in a period of transition, the like of which is rare in the history of the world. It is a time of profound change which resembles the time of the Reformation; the dissolution of the Roman Empire; the fall of Jerusalem. Eras such as these have engendered what we call "Apocalyptic" or "Crisis" literature. And so many today are looking to the Book of Revelation for keys, for answers to the problems of our time. And this search is not unwarranted. While there are many abuses in the interpretation of the Book of Revelation, it seems that God, Himself, is directing people to this book. Many all over the world are receiving prophecies about end times; they are receiving passages from the Book of Revelation, from the apocalypses of the Synoptic Gospels and so on, all of which focus attention on so-called apocalyptic literature.

Christians world-wide are currently reading passages and teachings from Matthew 24, Luke 21, Mark 13, and Ezekiel; also, over and over again, prophecies are being received warning us to be ready, to be watchful, to be prepared for whatever God might be saying or doing at any moment. In addition, one hears all kinds of teachings and talks about "the rapture." People have signs on the backs of their cars: "Are you ready for the rapture?" They see, in the Book of Revelation, prophecies for our times, prophecies about Russia, Red China, about what's going to happen in 1978 or 1984. I think a lot of this is misused. There's so

12

much discussion about such a little understood subject, that tremendous confusion has been created. But along with the spreading use of the Book of Revelation, there's a lot of fear, growing fear, about reading and interpreting it because of this confusion.

While there is a good deal of abuse, there's also some very fine insight, too, and I don't want to undermine that. We live in a parallel era to the times depicted in the Book of Revelation, crisis times, and so it is helpful for us to learn from this first century book what we might appropriately apply to our day.

Another valuable feature of The Book of Revelation is the good picture it gives of first century Church life. This may seem strange to some for not many look at it from this angle. When we want to examine first century Church life, we usually turn to the Acts of the Apostles. But the Book of Revelation is also an excellent guide to first century church life. I remember giving a course in Church history a few years ago in a college. I wanted to illustrate church life in the first century, and so, in the first semester we studied the Acts of the Apostles and in the second turned to the Book of Revelation. The students were stunned to see the insights that the second book offered to a clear knowledge of first century Church life. The difficulties, problems and resolutions of this century have a lot of relevance for our own time. This, I suggest, is an excellent use for the Book of Revelation: to study first century Church life to learn how we might effectively act in our troubled times.

This isn't the usual use of the Book of Revelation, though. We see how it is ordinarily used in the popular literature on Revelation, the popular radio talks, and the popular television broadcasts. This approach demonstrates in general a rather poor biblical understanding of the Book of Revelation, because it is seen as pure prophecy rather than as apocalyptic-type literature.

Many evangelists treat the book as source material for current prophecy about twentieth-century events. They see China and Russia depicted in the pages of this book, for example: they predict, from its pages, what will happen in 1980, what will happen in Jerusalem and in the Arab world, in the United Nations, in the Roman Catholic Church (often seen as Rome, the Babylon of Revelation). This kind of understanding prompts people to see the book as purely prophetic. They look for modern applications and miss much of the original content. According to sound biblical scholarship, this book is primarily about first century Church life, just as Jeremiah is about sixth century B.C. life in Israel, and Ezekiel about the time of the Exile in Israel. Once we understand this, and grasp the original meaning, we can see by extension how the message of these books might apply to our time.

My thesis is that the Book of Revelation is at least ninety-five per cent concerned with the events of the first and second centuries. So instead of being a prophetic book for our times, it's a book mostly about past history where we might see applications and parallels and learn a good deal for ourselves. However, we are not going to find pure prophecy about Russia or Red China.

Part One

Biblical Background
to
the Book of Revelation

1 Matthew 24 and the Fall of Jerusalem

Let us refer to some helpful sources to see this book as it should be seen in its historical context. I'd like to begin by studying with you the twenty-fourth chapter of Matthew which is called the Apocalypse of Matthew. "Apocalypse," incidently, is a word meaning the same thing as "revelation". It's a Greek word for the pulling back of the veil, the revealing, the revealing of secrets, of a mystery that people miss. The apostles had asked Jesus what he meant when He spoke about the destruction of the temple. Jesus explained in this long discourse of Matthew 24. I think our understanding of this passage and the parallels in Mark and Luke will help us immensely in our understanding of the Book of Revelation. It's the same type of literature, apocalyptic literature.

Let's start with verse 5 of chapter 24. Jesus said, "Be on guard! Let no one mislead you." This is a very interesting observation. "Many will come attempting to impersonate me. 'I am the Messiah!' they will claim, and they will deceive many. You will hear of wars and rumors of wars. Do not be alarmed. Such things are bound to happen, but that is not yet the end. Nation will rise against nation, one kingdom against another. There will be famine and pestilence and earthquakes in many places. These are the early stages of the birth pangs." Note this last sentence; it is extremely important. *These are the early stages of the birth pangs.* It is not about an end of the world but

17

rather about birth pangs. "They will hand you over to torture and kill you. Indeed, you will be hated by all nations on my account. Many will falter then, betraying and hating one another. False prophets will rise in great numbers to mislead many. Because of the increase of evil, the love of most will grow cold. The man who holds out to the end, however, is the one who will see salvation. This good news of the kingdon will be proclaimed throughout the world as a witness to all the nations. Only after that will the end come. When you see the abominable and destructive thing which the prophet Daniel foretold standing on holy ground (let the reader take note!), those in Judea must flee to the mountains. If a man is on the roof terrace, he must not come down to get anything out of his house. If a man is in the field, he must not turn back to pick up his cloak. It will be hard on pregnant or nursing mothers in those days. Keep praying that you will not have to flee in winter or on a sabbath, for those days will be more filled with anguish than any from the beginning of the world until now or in all ages to come. Indeed, if the period had not been shortened, not a human being would be saved. For the sake of the chosen, however, the days will be shortened. If anyone tells you at the time, 'Look, the Messiah is here,' or 'He is there,'; so if they tell you, 'Look He is in the desert,' do not believe it. False messiahs and false prophets will appear, performing signs and wonders so great as to mislead even the chosen if that were possible. Remember, I have told you all about it beforehand,' do not go out there; or, 'He is in the innermost rooms,' do not believe it. As the lightning from the east flashes to the west, so will the coming of the Son of Man be. Where the carcass lies, there the vultures gather. Immediately after the stress of that period, 'the sun will be darkened, the moon will not shed her light, the stars will fall from the sky, and the hosts of heaven will be shaken loose. Then the sign of the Son of Man will appear in the sky, and 'all the clans of earth will strike their breasts' as they see 'the Son of Man coming on the clouds of heaven' with power and great glory. He will dispatch his angels 'with a mighty trumpet blast and they will assemble his chosen from the four winds, from one end of the heavens to the other.' From the fig tree learn a lesson.'' Note this passage, too, it is very important. "When its branch grows tender and sprouts leaves, you realize that summer is near. Likewise, when you see all these things happening, you will know that he is near, standing at your door. I assure you, ''-and this is the real key to the passage - *''the present generation* will not pass away until all this takes place. The heavens and the earth will pass away but my words will not pass.''

Let us review this passage and see what Jesus is saying through the clues that I pointed out to you in the foregoing. The first clue I underlined was, "when this happens. . . look on it as the *birth pangs* of something that is about to happen, a *new birth.''* The second clue I underlined for you was the example of springtime, fig trees sprouting leaves. You know that summer is near. It is a time to lift up your heads. Look up. Rejoice! It's hardly a sign of the end of civilization, the end of the world. And, finally, Jesus' real clue: "This generation will not pass away until all this takes place.'' Consequently, I think it's quite evident that Jesus is not talking about the end of the world. Even though from signs like the falling of the stars, the sun not shedding its light, the moon being darkened, it might seem that way. We'll take a look at some of those images a little later. But from these definite clues, you know that He's not talking about doom but about crisis, a transition. Jesus compares it, in the 16th chapter of St. John, to a woman about to bring forth a child. A woman in childbirth is in great pain.

But when the child is born, she forgets her pain for joy that a child is born into the world. This is a typical messianic image from the Old Testament, the travail of new birth in the Lord. And that's what He is talking about here. He is not talking about the end of the world; He is talking about the end of *a* world. And I think that's the key to the whole passage. He's talking about the end of a world of Judaism that was missing the point, not recognizing its Messiah when He came. This made Jesus weep. As He talked about the destruction of Jerusalem, He was in tears. He was in great sorrow over "not a stone being left upon a stone," a division of Roman armies coming and encircling the city, destroying it because it did not know the hour of its visitation. Jerusalem would not, like little chicks, let the mother hen welcome it under her wings.

And Jesus tearfully told about the end of this civilization, this particular type of civilization that so characteristically ended when the veil of the Temple was split in two while Jesus, the Messiah, died on Calvary. This marked the end of a world, the world of Judaism, whose mission it had been to bring forth the Messiah. And yet, at that very moment, a new birth was taking place. The *real* Israel was being born out of the side of the new Adam pierced on the cross, as our Patristic tradition shows us so beautifully. It was the end of a world that had rejected the Messiah. In the year seventy A.D., Roman armies encircled Jerusalem and destroyed it. This is what Jesus meant: the end of a world, but at the same time, the beginning — the birth of a new world. It was the fulfillment of God's promises about the true Israel, the Israel of faith.

Jesus, when He was before the Sanhedrin and the High Priest at the time of His trial, said something very similar to this passage. When asked if He were the Son of God, He said Yes. "And you will see the

Son of Man (image from Daniel) coming on the clouds of heaven in power and majesty." *(Dan. 7)* What He meant was that even though He was mostly silent during the trial, in that judgement, you will see reality someday. You will see in the heavens the Son of Man vindicated. You will see the birth of a new world. You will see God. You will see the Messiah stirring, as Daniel prophesied, coming in the heavens to inaugurate a new world. And you will see it in this generation!

So that's what this passage means. It is entirely about the destruction of Jerusalem, the destruction of a Judaism that failed to recognize and receive its messiah. And yet out of that pain, which would be childbirth, a new world, a new Israel would be born, the Israel of faith with Jesus as Lord, coming on the clouds over the whole world in power and majesty to inaugurate a new type of existence. The kingdom of God in-breaking upon earth! This is what this passage is about: the fall of Jerusalem, the end of Judaism and the birth of Christianity, the new and real Jerusalem, the Israel on high.

We will now move into some of the background study that Jerome did in order to understand other passages of the Bible. Before we approach the text of the Book of Revelation, however, I will offer a few more comparative studies such as I did in Matthew.

2 Isaiah 13 and the Fall of Babylon

Let's turn now to the 13th chapter of Isaiah, an apocalyptic section. Let's read it. There are some very interesting lines here. We shall start around verse 6. Note that the title of this section is "Oracle against Babylon." Babylon was *the* power in the world at that time, something like Russia would be today, or the United States. Babylon was the sole big power of the world, had conquered Israel and was the ruling authority when Isaiah had this prophecy from the Lord about her. Just about Babylon! Just about the fall of Babylon. But note the imagery, the terminology of this passage. You will see many similarities to the passage quoted in Matthew 24.

"Howl, for the day of the Lord is near," (I'll say more on the "day of the Lord" later.) " . . . as destruction from the Almighty it comes. Therefore all hands fall helpless, the bows of the young men fall from their hands. Every man's heart melts in terror." And note this next line: " . . . pangs and sorrows take hold of them, like a woman in labor they writhe." Note the image of transition from death to birth. This would refer to the fall of Babylon and the birth of hope for Israel. "They look aghast at each other, their faces aflame. Lo, the day of the Lord comes cruel, with wrath and burning anger; to lay waste the land and destroy the sinners within it!" Note this next section especially: "The stars and the constellations of the heavens send forth no light; The sun is dark when it rises, and the light of the moon does not shine." All these images about the heavens being moved are actually just about the fall of Babylon. In other words there is revealed, with poetic imagery, something like this: when God stirs, when He is disgusted with the way men are acting in the world, when He decides to interrupt the course of history and be the Lord of history, when He bestirs Himself across the Heavens or, as Jesus said, when "He comes on the clouds with power and majesty," He kicks up the clouds, the sun more or less gets out of the way with the glory of the Lord coming. The moon is darkened and the stars pale into insignificance with the stirring of the Lord. We are dealing with poetic imagery in order to describe the Lord stirring across the heavens. And He was just dealing with Babylon! All that imagery! One finds the same kind of imagery concerning the fall of Jerusalem and the fall of Rome later on. So note that we are not talking about the end of *the* world, however, we are speaking very much about the end of *a* world. The end of civilization, the end of a Babylonian world that terrorized the world at large. Let's read on.

"Thus I will punish the world for its evil and the wicked for their guilt." The world mentioned here is Babylon. In a poetic hyperbole, the whole world here is the Babylonian world. "I will put an end to the pride of the arrogant, the insolence of tyrants I will humble. I will make mortals more rare than pure gold, men than gold of Ophir. For this I will make the heavens tremble and the earth shall be shaken from its place." Note the imagery. "The earth shall be shaken from its place." This is merely a reference to the fall of Babylon. "At the wrath of the Lord of hosts on the day of his burning anger. Like a hunted gazelle, or a flock that no one gathers, every man shall turn to his kindred and flee to his own land. Everyone who is caught shall be run through; to a man, they shall fall by the sword.

Their infants shall be dashed to pieces in their sight; their houses shall be plundered and their wives ravished." One notes the similarity here of this imagery to that of the woe of pregnant mothers in that day. For the imagery, typically, is about disaster coming, a nation falling and everybody having to run for their lives and, of course, it's harder for pregnant women to run than it is for young men. Jesus is drawing from this tradition of Israel to talk about this same kind of imagery when He describes the coming fall of Jerusalem. Isaiah says the same thing about the fall of Babylon. We are in a parallel crisis.

3 The Book of Judith

Let us examine some more apocalyptic literature from the Old Testament, the Book of Judith. One may not consider Judith a very apocalyptic book but it is. We do not have the scholarship to appreciate this, and so we miss the point of the book. Let me provide a little background.

The story is concerned with extremely troubled times, also a rather *vague* time. In fact, it's very difficult to pinpoint the exact period of time the book of Judith is dealing with because it's rather fictional. The story is about Nebuchadnezzer, the tyrant, who is pictured as the Assyrian King even though in reality he was a Babylonian. He is portrayed as an Assyrian King because Assyria happened to be the archetypal enemy of Israel and Nebuchadnezzer the archetypal villain. It was he who captured Jerusalem in 587 B.C., which makes him the villain par excellence. Thus, in Judith, Nebuchadnezzer is made into an Assyrian. He's waging war against Arphaxad, an unknown Median King, mentioned nowhere else in scripture or history. And he has an army commanded by a Persian called Vagoo. Now, to understand the meaning of all this, you will have to engulf several centuries, several different empires, all made to look as if there was one big battle against Israel. It would be the equivalent,

Peter Ellis* writes, of our saying: "An army commanded by the Russian, Peter the Great who is King of England, waging war with Arphaxad, King of France, with any army led by Generals Eisenhower and MacArthur." That's really what the book of Judith is saying. And Judith, of course, is a pseudonym; it simply means "the Jewess" or Lady Israel, the virgin Israel, or Mother Israel, protected by her God against overwhelming enemies in days of great crisis. It's a fictional story obviously written to bolster the hopes of people in times of crisis. An example of such a crisis might be at the time of Antiochus IV, when the nation was being plundered, Jerusalem being captured, and the Temple being destroyed. This is what we call apocalyptic literature, crisis literature, or a major transitional-period of history literature.

*Ellis, Peter, Men and the Message of the Old Testament. (Liturgical Press, 1962) p. 523

4 The Book of Daniel

Let us examine finally, in our pursuit of early apocalyptic types, the book of Daniel. Many believe that Daniel is a prophetic book. In fact, it is listed among the prophets in the Bible. But in reality, Daniel is not a prophetic book. In the original Hebrew Canon, Daniel came after the book of Esther and not after the book of Ezekiel where it would have come if it were a prophetic book. It's listed among the historical books of Hebrew literature. However, it pretends to be a prophetic book from about the fifth or sixth century B.C. but there is absolutely no reference to the book of Daniel anywhere in Hebrew literature before the year 175 B.C. No reference to it in parallel literature, no biblical allusions, no knowledge of a Daniel before this period. So you can see, it couldn't have appeared later than the year 175. This gives us a clue as to what the book is all about, with its famous seventy weeks of "prophecy" about the coming of the Messiah and the destruction of the Temple, and so forth. Yet many view it today as prophetic literature when it isn't. All attempts to end the seventy weeks of Daniel with Mussolini, Hitler, Red China, Russia, and Arab countries are misguided. Daniel is really apocalyptic literature written to bolster the faith and the assurance of the people of Israel at the time of the Hellenistic invasion. As much an enemy as Nebuchadnezzer, who destroyed Jerusalem in 587, was Antiochus IV who committed the famous "abomination of desolation," when he took the Temple of Jerusalem and profaned it, putting in that Temple the statue of Zeus.

27

This was a catastrophe to the Jewish people! This was the worst thing that could ever happen to them. Their hope and faith were shaken. Daniel was inspired by God as a book of hope in times of tremendous crisis to give the people, the Jews, assurance that their laws would crush all empires and that their God would right this wrong and restore Israel.

So Daniel like Judith, was made to seem like a prophetic forecast, something one might see on a television or hear on radio, a historical recreation of a scene. A kind of "you are there" program. To show the people of 175 B.C. in Israel that God was very much in command of history and not the Hellenists, not Antiochus IV, they have this story foretold as coming from the mouth of an ancient sage, a man named Daniel (of whom, incidentally, there is no historical evidence at all). The story is told by Daniel talking between the fifth and sixth century B.C., the Babylonian Exile up to the present time of around 175 B.C., in terms of seventy weeks where it pictures event after event in the course of those seventy weeks leading up to a great catastrophe. The point of the book is that God is in charge, even though there's been an "abomination of desolation." The rub is that it is an abomination that the Lord would avenge, that Israel would rebound from. That's the story of Daniel. It is meant to convey this kind of message: "Israelites, don't panic. God is in charge. He's always won. We'll win again. He's on our side. Even if the temple is destroyed, God has from the past always been victorious and He's going to do it again." The rest of the book tells the ancient stories of heroes that led Israel to victory in the past. It's an apocalyptic book. It's entirely about the famous three and one-half years of terrible persecution under Antiochus IV, roughly around 175 B.C. In fact, the famous three and one-half years of terrible persecution become the archetypal time, if you will, of all future persecution. Whether you call it forty-two months, 1,260 days, or three and a half years, you'll see all of these images in the book of Revelation. They all have to do with that original period of tremendous crisis around 175 B.C. And that little period of three and a half years is seen as the archetypal period of all suffering for the Lord.

5 Characteristics of Apocalyptic Literature

We have dealt with the historical background on apocalyptic literature. Now we can begin to define apocalyptic literature.

It always appears against a background of persecution, suffering, transition — transition from one period of history to another, the process of which is likened to the birth pangs of a new world. It is a literature designed to give assurance of faith to people undergoing tremendous trials. It is a resistance literature. It is often coated with a sort of military code so the enemy won't understand it. Only the initiate, the people of Israel, will really understand. It thrived, particularly in the period between 200 B.C. and 200 A.D. This was a period of four hundred years of great crisis in Israel and in the whole world. There are all kinds of apocalyptic literature in that period, both inside and outside the Bible. In the Bible, there are the books already mentioned: Daniel, Judith, sections of Ezekiel, Isaiah, Zachariah, Joel, and then, in the New Testament, the apocalypses of Matthew, Mark, and Luke, plus the Book of Revelation. Outside of the Bible, there are all kinds of apocalypses like the Apocalypse of Moses, the Apocalypse of Ezra, the Apocalypse of Baruch, of Henoch, the Psalms of Solomon, the Odes of Solomon. All are examples of apocalyptic crisis literature, offered to sustain hope in times of tremendous stress. Confronted by one empire or another, little Israel was buffeted this way and that. Likewise, the Christian martyrs of the first two centuries were almost wiped out by the Jews and then by the Romans, by emperors, governors of provinces and so forth. Such periods of history engendered various types of apocalyptic literature.

Apocalyptic literature, as we have said, is often coded and therefore full of symbols. We'll make further note of that a little later as we examine some of the examples in the Book of Revelation. It's a symbolic literature that keeps rummaging through the past to give assurance of hope for the present. In fact, we might say there was developed an "apocalyptic arsenal" or storehouse of images, a storehouse of apocalyptic weaponry. An array of stageprops, if you will, from past difficulties, past moments of God's victory is dug into over and over again to bring out the weapons of present defense and victory. It's not so much historical literature, although it's deeply historical, but rather trans-historical or "meta-historical." Let me talk of the metaphysical, that is — below and deeper than the *seeming* historical. For example, enemies in the Book of Revelation are *directly* God and Satan. The battleground of men, Romans and Christians almost disappears and one is left with the deep reality of a direct conflict between God and Satan which is at the root of history. Jesus calls Satan the Prince of this world and the enemy. And Paul tells us our battle is "not against human forces but against the principalities and powers." *(Eph.6:10)* Apocalyptic literature gets right down to the bone, under the surface. It gets right down to the confrontation of Christ's temptation in the desert — the real conflict between God and Satan in the destinies of nations and of individuals where always God slays the dragon and men are rescued from the latter's clutches. Men are seen as pawns in the battle between God and Satan, but not as helpless pawns; rather pawns that are in the hands of a loving God. They must choose to be on God's side and win the battle with the grace of the Savior. So it's deeply historical but not the usual kind of history. It's deep-down history, trans-historical, "meta-historical" reality, apocalyptic literature. It looks beyond emperors and kings. That's why the Book of Judith could speak of an Assyrian leader who is really a Babylonian fighting against an unknown Mede with Persian help. It really didn't matter much. The key factor was God, as the Lord of History, crushing all His enemies, the Lord defeating Satan and all his minions. It little mattered who were the cast of characters. The historical scene could blind one to the deeper trans-historical reality of the battle between God and Satan.

6 The "Apocalyptic Arsenal"

We have examined some of the characteristics of apocalyptic literature. I'd like to consider, at this point, what I call the "apocalyptic arsenal," the collection of stage props that are trotted out repeatedly in this kind of literature. The pregnant woman running, the birth pains, the Day of the Lord, all of these and others, what is their source? Let us examine some biblical background of apocalyptic origins that provide keys to our understanding of the Book of Revelation.

The first collection of weapons in this "arsenal," can be traced to Exodus 7-12: the plagues in Egypt, the locusts, the innundation of the Nile River, the death of the first born, and so forth; God used the weapons against Pharaoh to set Israel free from Egypt. Pharaoh is seen as an archetypal enemy of God, a symbol of Satan, if you will, keeping men in bondage. Anytime that God wants to work a tremendous liberation, a setting free of His people, the biblical author will reach into the past, into remembrance of Egypt, and ask the Lord to send these plagues again to attack the enemy with an invasion of locusts, the reddening of the waters of the river, or whatever. And God is seen to have used these same weapons against Babylon and against Jerusalem, itself, when it rejected the Messiah.

The second type of weaponry is found in the covenant that the Lord made at Sinai with His people Israel amidst lightning, thunder, smoke, and storm clouds and trumpet blasts. All of these become stereo-type stage props for future great events, where the Lord would dramatically intervene in history, employing one or another of these to rescue His people, or to quell an enemy invasion.

The next stage prop is from Deuteronomy 28, the long list of blessings and curses, ten times worse than the plagues of Egypt, that the Lord, through Moses, threatened His people with if they disobeyed His covenant in the land into which they were going. These blessings and these curses are brought out repeatedly in apocalyptic literature to warn about events that might occur as a result of infidelity.

Another prop, a very famous one, is from Amos 5:18 where the first reference in the Bible to "the day of the Lord," is made which originally had to do with the fall of Samaria in 722 B.C. After Amos had warned these people of the North that, unless they returned to Yahweh, they would fall, he warned them "the day of the Lord" was going to come for them if they didn't listen. Samaria would be no more. They didn't listen to Amos, of course, and that "day of the Lord" did come. Samaria fell in 722 B.C. Amos had said something like "You're going to get it," and they did "get it." Accordingly this "day of the Lord" became a famous epithet, a famous slogan for all future days of the Lord when God would save Israel or destroy an enemy. Prophets would say, "You're going to get it, Nineveh," "You're going to get it, Rome. You're going to have your day." The Lord says even to Israel, "The day of the Lord might come for you, like an enemy, not a friend." The "day of the Lord" becomes a typical apocalyptic phrase.

The next stage prop is from Ezekiel 38 and 39: the famous apocalyptic battle between Gog and Magog and the forces of God, or the forces of anti-God against the forces of God. Israel was in exile at this time. The writings of Ezekiel are from this period. He talks about a cosmic battle between God and the enemies of God. Nobody knows the identities of Gog and Magog. They're merely fictional names for the archetypal enemies of God. These famous battles of Ezekiel 38 and 39, where the forces of anti-God battle the forces of God, are the source of many biblical images. The battle of Armageddon originates from here; it was originally a battle on the plains of Israel in a place called Megiddo, where Deborah and Barak fought in the book of Judges. Later Josiah, a good king of Israel, fell there. It was a tragic day for Israel. Subsequently, any great battle and defeat for Israel would be referred to as Megiddo, or Armageddon, where the forces of God would do battle against the forces of anti-God.

Other apocalyptic imagery stems from Isaiah 11 where the paradisiacal splendor of Genesis is found: the oasis, the Garden of Eden, fruit-bearing trees, the side of the river bearing fruit every month of the year, the Tree of Life. There is also the bear lying down with the cow, the lamb with the lion, the infant playing with the cobra. All these images become images of paradisiacal splendor when God's kingdom will come in apocalyptic times.

Other images from this arsenal are from Isaiah 13 and other similar passages that discuss the sun being shaken along with the moon and the stars, women fleeing who are pregnant, and the whole world coming to an end. All this imagery speaks of nothing more than the destruction of Babylon, the end of *a* world, the world of Babylon!

The next section of apocalyptic imagery comes from Zechariah, the prophet. I should rather say the apocalyptic writer, Zechariah. He uses a lot of imagery, some of which is found in Revelation: the famous horns, for example. Horns coming from animals like the ram are a symbol of power. Then there are the seven eyes of Zechariah, "seven" introducing a factor that is very popular in the Book of Revelation: the use of symbolic numbers. Seven is the symbol of perfection of fullness. Seven eyes symbolizing omniscience, that is someone who sees everything, God.

Then there are the four horsemen, "four" is a number that signifies universal: North, South, East, and West. God's angels are in the four corners of the world, all of which suggests God's providence over the whole world, four horsemen doing God's work as His messengers.

Another Zecharian image is the woman in the basket, a symbol of wickedness, who incidentally is transported to Babylon. It is important to note the connection between that and the famous scarlet woman of Revelation 17 and 18 in Babylon. Here a symbol of wickedness is transported to Babylon, an already symbolic city in Zechariah. In the Book of Revelation it is a symbolic city which is decoded as Rome.

Then there are the visions of Zechariah through which the Lord shows him the unfolding of history.

Another type of stage prop is taken from Job. The name "Job" is a pseudonym used for the hero of the book. Who is this Job? This book is similar to the Book of Judith. It is didactic fiction. Job is a fictional story, something like our *Rip Van Winkle* of American tradition. It teaches a lesson, just as Judith did. For example, Job isn't even an Israelite. Examined carefully, he was a wise man from the land of Hus. Hus, for an Israelite, would be something like the land of Arabian Nights to us. Job is from the mysterious land of Hus. "Job" is a pseudonym. It's a famous name out of legend, that would show a typical wise man acting, a legendary old sage. And history, lessons of history, are built around this man. To give these lessons an element of interest, a famous name is used as in Daniel and Judith.

Conclusion

So much for the "apocalyptical arsenal." We are now prepared to examine the Book of Revelation itself, and to begin to understand its original meaning.

First of all, it is not a book of prophecy. It is an apocalyptic book, a literature of crisis. This is where most people make their mistake, not having had the benefit of biblical scholarship. Accordingly, the book is often falsely interpreted as prophetic, rather than apocalyptic. People in this dilemma try, for example, to interpret all history in terms of those seventy weeks of Daniel, instead of seeing them as the literary device intended, namely, to give hope to the people living at 175 B.C. when the seventieth week was up. People who view the Book of Revelation as prophetic divide the history of the world into seven periods representing the letters to the seven churches; they do this because they see it as prophetic and not apocalyptic. They are trying to see in present life today, the realization of a book that really was almost entirely about the first and second century! So it's very important that we see this book for what it is.

At the beginning of this book, I quoted the warning from Deuteronomy and the end of Revelation. "Woe to anyone who adds to the writing of this book, or who subtracts from it." I would venture to say that to make the Book of Revelation say something it doesn't say is to add to the book. To see it as a prophetic book in its essence, its original meaning, is to add to the literal meaning of that book. It was not designed to be mainly prophetic. It was designed to give hope to the people of the first and second centuries fighting against the persecutions of Rome. The immediate background is the oppression of the Roman Empire, the persecutions of emperors like Nero and Domitian who were trying to eliminate the Christian Church. The enemy has switched from the high priest and the Sanhedrin trying to exterminate the Lord Jesus, to Nero and the emperors persecuting Peter and Paul and the early Christians, the martyrs of the first centuries. Rome is the arch-enemy: Nebuchadnezzer, Antiochus IV. The Roman Empire is the Babylon that the Old Testament talks about in its archetypal form.

Today, however, many do take this book prophetically. Since some have very great influence, as a result people are misled by it. This points to the problem surrounding great people like certain famous preachers and evangelists hearing prophetic words of apocalyptic messages for our times. I have no doubt about the authenticity of their message. However, they often inadvertently misinterpret the message, largely because of insufficient biblical scholarship. For example, in their tradition this Book of Revelation is prophetic, and the Rome of prophecy is often the Rome of today, the Rome of the Catholic Church. In much of fundamentalist biblical teaching, the whore of Babylon is the Roman Catholic Church whereas, in reality, it is the Roman Empire that was persecuting Christians in the first, second, and third centuries. If you view it as prophetic, you might well see it as Rome today. If you see it as apocalyptic, you can put it in right perspective and see it as all worldly empires like Rome fighting against Christians.

The degree of biblical background influences one's interpretation of this book. A fundamentalist approach vitiates a prophecy like a famous "vision" which has so much truth in it. It really was an authentic prophecy and I have no quarrel with it. I do quarrel, however, with the interpretation of that prophecy because of what I consider to be seemingly insufficient biblical background.

Now let us proceed with the Book of Revelation itself. The rest of this material concentrates on the specific background, to what the author is addressing himself and what the Holy Spirit is inspiring. We have to examine the intent of the book and the audience it was originally addressing. It is dated, most authors agree, about the period 81 to 90 A.D., under the Roman Emperor Domitian when terrible persecutions were being waged against Christians.

This persecution, of course, is felt to have a more profound meaning. It's seen as Satan trying to wipe out the Kingdom of Jesus Christ, the early budding Church trying to be born in the midst of a pagan world. It is a trans-historical or a "meta-historical" theme, written to bolster the hope of Christians who were going to their deaths in the arenas, who were undergoing fantastic suffering. It is to give them renewed joy and reassurance of victory.

It is important to keep this background in mind because of the coded form, destined to be distributed to Christians. If, for example, they were caught with the book by the Romans, they would probably be in immediate trouble. Apocalyptic literature exists in times of warfare to sustain people via a message they need to hear and which the enemy doesn't need to hear.

I would reaffirm again that the events of this book are at least ninety-five per cent consummated at the end of the first or second century, or at least by the fall of Rome as a pagan empire in 313 A.D. Just as the Apocalypses of Matthew, Mark, and Luke were concerned with the fall of Jerusalem, the beginning of a new world, with Jesus coming on the clouds as Lord to take over and renew society by the power of the Holy

Spirit, with the Body of Christ becoming the new Israel, so the Book of Revelation is parallel in terms of the Roman Empire. Just as the fall of Babylon and of Jerusalem took place, the author of Revelation assures Christians who are going to their death, that Rome, itself, will fall. God is going to stir across the clouds again. Jesus is going to come as He did in Jerusalem, in power and might. He will do so through His agents, the nations that work for Him such as the Parthians and the Medes, and plague and pestilence, and death and all the tools in His arsenal. Jesus is going to come across the clouds again in power and majesty, overthrow Satan and his minions, dethrone the Roman Empire and inaugurate·the Kingdom. "The kingdom of the world now belongs to our Lord and to His Christ!" *(Rev.11:15)* That's probably the key line in the Book of Revelation.

Again, it is apocalyptic literature, even though it poses as prophetic. It is destined to bring hope to people through the assurance of God's victory. The victory is going to come and come soon.

Part Two

The Book Of Revelation

1 The Setting

Having examined some necessary background to help us understand apocalyptic literature, let us now examine the text itself and explain some of the more difficult parts. Let us first look at Chapter One, the setting.

"This is the revelation (apocalypse) God gave to Jesus Christ, so that he might show his servants what must happen very soon." In other words, "lift up your heads, hang on, it will come soon." "He made it known by sending His angel", just as in Ezekiel God used an angel to speak to His people, to tell them when they were not even a nation, when they were in exile, that they could make plans about a new Jerusalem, a new nation. That same angel appears here; informed Israelites will remember and perceive the connection to the angel of Ezekiel, the prophetic angel announcing good tidings.

"(God sent) his angel to his servant John, who in reporting all he saw bears witness to the word of God and the testimony of Jesus Christ. Happy is the man who reads this prophetic message." Note that it is called a prophetic message. It poses as such even though in reality it is an apocalyptic message. "Happy are those who hear it and heed what is written in it, for the appointed time is near!

"To the seven Churches in the province of Asia; John wishes you grace and peace — from Him who is and who was and who is to come." That's God the Father. "And from the seven spirits before his throne." That is the Holy Spirit, the seven-fold Spirit of God, the Spirit that is life, abundance, fullness. "And from Jesus Christ the faithful witness." The Trinity is complete now, Father, Spirit and Son. "The first born from the dead and ruler of the kings of earth. To him who loves us and freed us from our sins by his own blood, who has made us a royal nation of priests in the service of his God and Father — to him be glory and power forever and ever! Amen."

Now the very apocalyptic prophecy: "See, he comes amid the clouds!" When the early Christians prayed, "Come, Lord Jesus," that's what they meant! Come on the clouds, bestir Yourself and come across the heavens and right this world! Like Daniel's "Son of Man" *(Dan.7)* coming on the clouds. "See, he comes amid the clouds! Every eye shall see him, even of those who pierced him. All the peoples of the earth shall lament him bitterly. So it is to be! Amen!"

The Lord is coming to make a new world, a world where He will be Lord of all.

Now look at the next line. It provides a good clue. "I, John, your brother, who share with you the distress and the kingly reign and the endurance we have in Jesus . . ." There is the whole apocalyptic theme. "I share with you, my fellow Christians, the distress and the endurance we must have. But also the victories, the kingly reign we have in Jesus. Hold on, lift up your heads. The victory is coming. we are in the birth pains, like a woman who is about to give birth, of a new world. We are going to beat Rome. We and Jesus are going to overcome and make a new world where the Spirit will renew the face of the earth. John is writing this while in exile on an island called Patmos, a rocky island in the Aegean Sea. "Because I proclaimed God's word and bore witness to Jesus."

John was suffering tremendous distress while writing this, therefore it was written out of crisis. "On the

Lord's day I was caught up in ecstasy, and I heard behind me a piercing voice like the sound of a trumpet, which said, 'Write on a scroll what you see and send it to the seven churches'." The churches in question are churches of that area that John the Evangelist is commonly associated with. "I turned around to see whose voice it was that spoke to me. When I did so I saw seven lampstands of gold, and among the lampstands One like a Son of Man wearing an ankle-length robe, with a sash of gold about his breast." This imagery I will explain a little further. "The hair of His head was as white as snow white wool and his eyes blazed like fire. His feet gleamed like polished brass refined in a furnace, and his voice sounded like the roar of rushing waters. In his right hand he held seven stars. A sharp, two-edged sword came out of his mouth, and his face shone like the sun at its brightest."

One should not try to envision Jesus from these symbols! It would be a horrible picture of a man with a sword sticking out of his mouth to begin with! Rather, one should learn what apocalyptic imagery is. One has to decode or translate the image, and then one is left with a tremendous picture, the best picture of Jesus I've seen anywhere — truly beautiful. Let us translate the images as we go along.

First scenario: "Seven lampstands of gold, and among the lampstands One like a Son of Man." Let us examine these words. The seven lampstands, as we will see, are the seven churches. Remember the Gospel passage where Jesus says: "You are the light of the world?" Each church is supposed to be a light in the darkness, on a lampstand. So picture seven lampstands with seven churches around the circle. Now in the midst of the lampstands the Son of Man, Jesus, who lives in His Church, who is the Light of the world, stands. What the book is saying is that Jesus is the Light of the world. He is the Light of His Church. He is right in the midst of His lampstands, a beautiful picture. "Wearing an ankle-length robe." What does that mean? It means He is a Priest. He is the High Priest who wore ankle length robes. Read the book of Leviticus carefully. Jesus is the High Priest, the Priest offering sacrifice in the holy of holies. "With a sash of gold around his breast". What does that mean? It means He is a King. Kings wore gold sashes. So He is King of Kings and He is the High Priest and He lives in His Church. "The hair of his head was as white as snow-white wool." Does that mean an old man? No. On the contrary, He is going to be pictured in vigor, therefore young, strong. But white hair is a symbol of wisdom. Old men had white hair and a lot of wisdom, so Jesus has white hair. That means He is perfectly wise. "And his eyes blazed like fire." His eyes were sharp and saw everything. "His feet gleamed like polished brass refined in a furnace." He was strong, immutable. "And his voice sounded like the roar of rushing waters." He was powerful as the waters at flood tide; nothing could stop Him. Don't picture Jesus' voice like rushing water. Just understand the image of power. "In his right hand he held seven stars." The seven stars are the bishops, the heads, the presiding elders of each of the churches. And note that they are almost pawns in the hands of Jesus who is *The Shepherd*, *The Priest*. These leaders of the church are little stars, little lights in the hand of Jesus.

It's a beautiful image of a pastor, or shepherd. Everything is in the hands of the Lord. "A sharp two-edged sword came out of his mouth." This refers to the Word of God; the Word that was going to come forth from His mouth would cut like a two-edged sword, right to the heart of man. As Paul says, prophecy cuts right to the heart of man making him fall down on his knees and acknowledge that God has spoken. The Word of God cuts through everything. "And his face shone like the sun at its brightest." Jesus looked like this at the transfiguration. What a beautiful picture of the risen Lord Jesus! There couldn't be a better one.

"When I caught sight of him, I fell down at his feet as though dead. He touched me with his right hand and said: There is nothing to fear. I am the First and the Last and the One who lives. Once I was dead but now I live — forever and ever. I hold the keys of death and the nether world. Write down, therefore, whatever you see in visions — what you see now and will see in time to come." And then John begins his letters to the seven churches following from this initial vision of Jesus risen — Jesus risen, King of the world, he who later will open the scrolls and control history, Jesus risen from the dead after slaying the dragon, and who now is Lord of the world.

We will briefly examine the contents of the seven letters to the churches, and deal with highlights, difficult parts, and offer a word of explanation in the hope that the reader will be able to read the Book with more profit, the same kind of profit he could obtain from reading Jeremiah or the Gospel of Mark. That is the purpose of this book — to make the Book of Revelation, which many fear, available for use without any hesitation. It should not be taken for any more or less than what it says. If we could restore such equilibrium and approach it in the same way we approach the Gospel of John, without fear, we would have rendered a service and put this book back into good use for Christian people.

2 The Seven Letters to the Churches

The seven letters to the churches remind me of Paul's letters to the various churches, even though they are much shorter. They should be seen for the insights they give into first century Christianity — quick insights, but nonetheless revealing the life of the latter half of the first century. I think the letters are relatively easy to read, so I will merely choose some difficult passages and comment briefly.

The Letter to the Church at Ephesus. "I know your deeds, your labors, and your patient endurance. I know you cannot tolerate wicked men; you have tested those self-styled apostles who are nothing of the sort, discovered that they are imposters."

Just a word about "self-styled apostles." But first let's take note of similar phrases from the other letters. For example, a little further along in the letter to the church at Smyrna, "I know the slander you endure from self-styled Jews." Self-styled apostles in the first instance, self-styled Jews in the second instance. Now let's combine that with something else. "These men are nothing more than members of Satan's assembly. Have no fear of the sufferings to come."

Let us see what these verses mean. "Self-styled apostles." That's very much like one of the items Paul dealt with in his speech to the elders of Miletus in Acts 20 where he talks about "certain of your number who really never did belong to you in the first place, who have gone out and are causing trouble in the world." Non-sent apostles, self-styled apostles, who if you will pursue the Scriptures a bit further, are identified with the anti-christ, those who never really belonged to the Christian community. These are disruptive forces in the Christian body.

We now arrive at a point we discussed earlier: namely, that the Book of Revelation is "meta-historical" or trans-historical. It goes deep down into history; it is not the surface type of religion. That is why the battle is seen, not as a conflict between good and bad apostles, but between God and Satan: God working in the good apostles, Satan working in the self-styled ones. The battle is not seen as a conflict between the Church of Jesus and the synagogue, but rather as a battle between the Church of Jesus and the synagogue of Satan. The forces that oppose Jesus are here termed Satan's assembly. The battle is obviously more profound, that clear battle between God and Satan that characterizes apocalyptic literature.

John goes on to say, "The devil will indeed cast some of you into prison to put you to the test." There again one encounters the direct action of Satan working in history which characterizes this type of literature.

In that same first letter to Ephesus there's a reference to the practices of the "Nicolaitans." Who are these Nicolaitans?

In the letter to the church at Pergamum they mentioned again in this fashion: "Nevertheless, I hold a few matters against you: there are some among you who follow the teaching of Balaam, who instructed Balak to throw a stumbling block in the way of the Israelites by tempting them to eat food sacrificed to idols and to practice fornication. Yes, you too have those among you who hold to the teaching of the Nicolaitans."

A little later in the letter to the church at Thyatira we

find a section that is very similar. "Nevertheless I hold this against you: you tolerate a Jezebel — that self-styled prophetess." Here's another term, self-styled prophetess, just like self-styled apostles and self-styled Jews. The reality is that they are not Jews, not apostles, not a prophetess. They are like the non-sent prophets in the Christian community today. We are often plagued by prophets who aren't sent from any authoritative community or from God, but are self-sent with personal messages, causing havoc here and there.

This self-styled prophetess, Jezebel, is undoubtedly a Nicolaitan too, as in the other communities. All this that the author is warning about is the heresy of Nicholas. It is not really known who Nicholas was, except that his followers are called Nicolaitans. It involves a compromise with the world. The clue to that is in chapter 2, verse 14: a comparison with Balaam, a prophet in the Old Testament that plagued the Israelites. First of all, he couldn't curse the Israelites when King Balak wanted him to. Later on, however, he led the Israelites into a compromise by enticing them through Moabite women to adopt their religious practices of the land, and to forsake the pure Israelite worship they had vowed to the Lord. They fell victim to idolatry, intermarriage and the worship of the Moabites. The purity of the Israelite faith was thereby weakened and changed. In other words what Balaam did, Nicholas and his followers were doing to the early Christians. They were leading them into a compromise with the world, the same kind of compromise that Paul writes about. He calls it freedom become license, i. e., some people, in the guise of freedom, actually have fallen victim to license. They feel that they can worship God and yet live more or less the ways of the pagans around them. We find them, for example, eating food sacrificed to idols and giving scandal, plus taking part in temple worship that is commanded by the kings and the emperors. They were keeping one foot in each world.

Paul dealt with the same struggle when he spoke about those who give scandal by eating food sacrificed to idols. He said he would rather go without meat the rest of his life than give scandal to a brother Jew. But there were those who didn't have the sensitivity of Paul. They usually had a gnostic bent that perceived religion as something purely spiritual; the body was not all that important in this view. In one's mind one might follow the Lord but in one's practice, in one's daily living out of life in the body, one might actually live like the pagans. Keep them happy. Such a dangerous compromise, such intellectual snobbery held that flesh is bad and the spirit alone is worthy; it eventually even denied that Jesus came in the flesh, as John writes in his Epistle. The Gnostics were "superspiritual"; they believed that Jesus, and a good Christian, are solely "of the spirit." The flesh by itself, mattered little so it made no difference whether one indulged in the emperor worship of the surrounding people as long as one knew who Jesus was and followed him "in spirit." This type of compromise was rampant in these churches. It was understandable, when one recalls that Christians were being put to death for refusing to take part in emperor worship. So there developed a group of Christians who did compromise, the Nicolaitans, and it was against them that the Evangelist here was raging.

In the aforementioned letter to the church at Pergamum John says: "I know you live in the very place where Satan's throne is erected." What does that mean: to have a throne erected to Satan? No. Again, it refers to the direct conflict between God and Satan, and here Satan is conceived as the force behind emperor worship. Pergamum was the seat of the Roman

Empire in the provinces, the seat of the governor. That is why it is called Satan's throne. The dragon, or the beast, is behind emperor worship so the throne is called "Satan's throne." It is like the above where it says, "The devil will indeed cast some of you into prison." Governors and judges will throw Christians into prison, but in the trans-historical, or "meta-historical" fashion, the devil, the adversary, is pictured as throwing Christians into prison.

So much for the letters except for one other point. At the end of the letter to the Ephesians we read: "Let him who has ears heed the Spirit's word to the churches! I will see to it that the victor eats from the tree of life which grows in the garden of God." Here is a reference to one of the stage props we spoke about previously. The imagery is from Genesis, the paradisiacal splendor of the garden, or Isaias 11 which talks about paradise restored. From the apocalyptic arsenal this image is conjured to show a paradise, a wholeness, restored to the Christian who endures to the end.

3 The Heavenly Scene

We will look at chapter 4 now, and then the body of the Book of Revelation itself. "After this I had another vision." Here is another apocalyptic tool, a vision. "Above me there was an open door to heaven, and I heard the trumpetlike voice which had spoken to me before. It said, 'Come up here and I will show you what must take place in time to come.' At once I was caught up in ecstasy. A throne was standing there in heaven, and on the throne was seated One whose appearance had a gemlike sparkle as of jasper and carnelian. Around the throne was a rainbow as brilliant as emerald." This description and many others that follow are taken directly out of the father of apocalyptic literature, Ezekiel. A similar description of God is found in chapters 1 and 10 of Ezekiel.

"Surrounding his throne were twenty-four other thrones upon which were seated twenty-four elders." Who are these twenty-four elders? It is a symbolic figure. We are going to be dealing frequently with numbers. Let us see what some of them represent. Twenty-four is from the twelve tribes of Israel plus the twelve Apostles. There is a beautiful merger of old and new, the new Israel coming right out of the trunk of the ancient Israel. The twenty-four elders, therefore, represent people of the Old and New Testaments who are faithful to the Lord and are now before his throne. "They were clothed in white garments and had crowns of gold on their heads." What is the symbolism here? White is used throughout this book and white means victory. We still use white for our baptismal robes. At Easter we have white in the liturgy to symbolize victory. White robes are the symbol of victory, just as a palm branch is the symbol of victory. Crowns of gold on their head is another symbol of victory.

"From the throne came flashes of lightning and peals of thunder." This recalls the scene at Sinai. These images come from the apocalyptic arsenal of the covenant of Sinai. They indicate the appearance or presence of God. "Before it burned seven flaming torches, the seven spirits of God." Seven, as we've said, means fullness and the seven spirits here are a way of describing the Holy Spirit. The Holy Spirit of God is there.

We have so far the Father and the Spirit. "The floor around the throne was a sea of glass that was crystal-clear." It's a picture of brilliance. "At the very center, around the throne itself, stood four living creatures." These are angels, spirits, at the service of the Lord. Four, as we saw, means universal, ready to go out all over the world: north, south, east and west. It is a number that means the same thing as catholic or universal, God's Kingdom for everybody.

Now who are these four living creatures? Don't try to picture them. You won't be able to. It is again symbolic imagery that we have here. These four living creatures were "covered with eyes, front and back." That means simply that they were all knowing. They had tremendous vision. They could see everything that God saw. They were granted the very vision of God. They could see inside and outside.

"The first creature resembled a lion, the second an ox, the third had the face of a man, while the fourth looked like an eagle in flight." Again, don't try to picture them. Each of the four living creatures had six wings and eyes all over, inside and out. This is very much like the Seraphim in Isaiah, chapter six.

Let us take a look at the number six. It means a little less than God for seven is perfection and it will always be God or someone to whom God gives a particularly divine characteristic. We are going to see, a little later, the devil characterized as six-six-six — the height of imperfection.

But to get back to the ox and the lion, what do they mean? They are symbols denoting certain characteristics. The lion is a symbol of royalty, the royalty of God. The kingly reign of God is shared by these spirits. The ox — the strength of an ox. The face of a man — the cleverness of man, the ability of man to rule the earth. Or the eagle in flight — symbol of soaring splendor, mysticism, if you will. These kinds of qualities reside in spiritual beings. Christian tradition often applies them to the four Evangelists: Matthew, Mark, Luke and John.

Matthew, the man, because he seems to talk a great deal about the Man Jesus. He gives special emphasis to the humanity of Christ.

Luke, the ox, because he depicts the sacrifice of Jesus.

Mark, the Lion, because this connotes strength and royalty. It's the symbol of Venice for example. The lion is the royal king, royal scion of Judah.

And finally, John, the eagle, because of the soaring mysticism of the fourth Gospel.

"Whenever these creatures give glory and honor and praise to the One seated on the throne, who lives forever and ever, the twenty-four elders (saints of the Old and New Testament) fall down before the One seated on the throne, and worship him who lives forever and ever. They throw down their crowns before the throne and sing: 'O Lord our God, you are worthy to receive glory and honor and power!'" The throwing down of the crowns means that they recognize that all of their gifts, all that they have, comes from the Lord and they give back their crowns. They give all that they have to the Lord in worship, adoration, and thanksgiving. Thus one sees the symbolic gesture of throwing their crowns before the Lord. We read in one of the prefaces to the Christian liturgy that God, in crowning His saints, crowns His own gifts.

4 The Lamb and the Scroll

Let us now consider the Scroll and the Lamb, chapter 5. So far in John's vision there had just been the Father and the Spirit in this heavenly scene. "In the right hand of the One who sat on the throne I saw a scroll." It is a scroll which is going to mean the future history of the times. "It had writing on both sides," therefore, a lot of writing. "And it was sealed with seven seals." God Himself sealed it. It is perfectly sealed. Nobody can break it. "Then I saw a mighty angel who proclaimed in a loud voice: 'Who is worthy to open the scroll and break its seals?' But no one in heaven or on earth or under the earth could be found to open the scroll or examine its contents. I wept bitterly because no one could be found worthy to open or examine the scroll. One of the elders said to me: 'Do not weep. The Lion of the tribe of Judah, the Root of David, has won the right by his victory to open the scroll with the seven seals.'"

The lamb now is seen as coming forward, the lion of the tribe of Judah, a lamb standing that had been slain. "He had seven horns and seven eyes; these eyes are the seven spirits of God sent to all parts of the world. The Lamb came and received the scroll from the right hand of the One who sat on the throne."

Let's review. The Lamb, of course, is Jesus, slain on Calvary, the Lamb of God who was to take away the sins of the world.

He is pictured as coming forward. Again, don't try to visualize this. All it means is that He is the Paschal

Lamb, by His death on the Cross. Seven horns mean that He has all power; the horn is the symbol of power. He had seven eyes which means that He was all seeing, omniscient. Immediately following these words, it says that the seven eyes are the seven spirits of God. Jesus possessed the Holy Spirit. He was able to give the Holy Spirit, to baptize with the Holy Spirit those to whom He wished to give the Spirit. The Lamb standing means that even though He was slain, He had risen from the dead and is standing now, victorious. He is walking up to the throne receiving all dominion and all power from the Father. The Gospel of John states that all judgement is given to the Son because He was the Son of Man. And when Jesus the Lamb now comes into the presence of the Father, all fall down and worship Him. The twenty-four elders fall down along with their harps. "The elders were holding vessels of gold filled with aromatic spices, which were the prayers of God's holy people."

The heavenly worship is seen as joined with the earthly worship, taking the prayers of God's holy people as incense before the throne. And this is the new hymn they sang: "Worthy are you to receive the scroll and break open its seals, for you were slain."

This means that Jesus is now the Lord of history! No one had the key to history; no one could unravel it. In fact, many people today are trying to discover what history is all about, what is the meaning of man, what is the meaning of the world.

The Book of Revelation is saying that Jesus alone has the key. He alone can unravel the scroll by His death and resurrection. He is the Lord of history. He gives the key of life to men. As He unrolls the scroll, He controls history and unravels the times for men. "His are the times and his are the ages," we say in the liturgy.

And then the scene is presented of all the angels and saints worshipping the Lamb along with the Father. It is a sure picture of the divinity of Jesus Christ.

5 The Seven Seals

Let us consider chapter 6. "Then I watched while
the Lamb broke open the first of the seven seals."
Jesus is now unravelling His victory, the meaning of
His victory obtained by His death and resurrection.
"(He) broke open the first of the seven seals, and I
heard one of the four living creatures (God's chief
lieutenants, if you will) cry out in a voice like thunder,
'Come forward!' To my surprise, I saw a white horse;
its rider had a bow, and he was given a crown. He
rode forth victorious, to conquer yet again. When the
Lamb broke open the second seal, I heard the second
living creature cry out, 'Come forward!' Another
horse came forth, a red one. Its rider was given power
to rob the Earth of peace by allowing men to slaughter
one another. For this he was given a huge sword.
When the Lamb broke open the third seal, I heard the
third living creature cry out: 'Come forward!' This
time I saw a black horse, the rider of which held a pair
of scales in his hand. I heard what seemed to be a voice
coming from in among the four living creatures. It
said: 'A day's pay for a ration of wheat and the same
for three of barley! But spare the olive oil and the
wine!' When the Lamb broke open the fourth seal, I
heard the four living creatures cry out, 'Come forward!' Now I saw a horse sickly green in color. Its
rider was named death, and the nether world was in
his train. These four were given authority over one-
quarter of the earth, to kill with sword and famine and
plague and the wild beasts of the earth.

"When the Lamb broke open the fifth seal, I saw under the altar the spirits of those who had been martyred because of the witness they bore to the Word of God. They cried out at the top of their voices: 'How long will it be, O Master, Holy and true, before you judge our cause and avenge our blood among the inhabitants of the earth?' Each of the martyrs was given a long white robe, and they were told to be patient a little while longer until the quota was filled of their fellow servants and brothers to be slain, as they had been."

Let us pause for a moment now, and see what the above means. The background of this book, as we said, is the terrible persecution going on at the end of the first century under Domitian and the other Roman emperors. This book was written to give assurance and hope to suffering Christians on earth. That is why in verse 9 and following, the prayer of the Saints on earth and the prayer of the martyrs in Heaven is going up before the throne of God saying, "When are you going to come and vindicate our cause? When are you going to come and judge our cause? We fought for you and here we are dead." The Lord is answering, "I'm coming. I'm coming soon to establish right on earth."

And as the Lamb unravels the seal, you see Him controlling history just as in the Old Testament where you have, for example, Cyrus called "the anointed of the Lord" as He came from Persia to set Jerusalem free and remake the nation. Or, as other emperors, he was used by God as a pawn to control the history of Israel. Here now you see the Lamb controlling various things, armies, for example. The white horse probably represents the Parthians, an army from the East coming to invade the Roman Empire and give a little rest to Christians.

The red horse means war. Red is the color of blood, warfare. It, too, is controlled by the Lord of history. It is warfare against the enemies of God to set the Christians free.

And then famine is seen as a weapon of God, famine signified by the black horse with the scales in his hand and wheat being rationed.

Then finally comes death itself, the sickly green horse. All happens at the command of the Lord. As He breaks open the seal, these things happen. They don't happen without God's signal, without His control. The Lamb is seen as opening the seal, in complete control, at every moment, of everything that happens. The whole purpose is to vindicate the saints, to establish the Kingdom of Christ on earth after the patient endurance and the suffering that martyrs are undergoing at the hands of the Roman Emperors.

Let us now consider verse 12. "When I saw the Lamb break open the sixth seal, there was a violent earthquake; the sun turned black as a goat's hair tent cloth, and the moon grew red as blood." You recognize now the imagery of Isaiah 13 that we discussed earlier, the imagery used for the fall of Babylon. In similar fashion the empire here, the Roman Empire, is being shaken. God is stirring across the Heavens. The sun is darkened, the moon loses its color, the stars fall, every time God stirs across the Heavens, every time the Son of Man comes on the clouds with power and majesty. This backdrop or stage prop from the apocalyptic arsenal, is displayed in the colorful imagery of the biblical writer.

So God is about to act, and His enemies are frightened — the kings of the earth, the nobles, and those in command, the wealthy and the powerful. "Those who engendered fear in the Christians all hid themselves in caves and mountain crags. They cried out to the mountains and the rocks: fall on us. Hide us from the face of the one who sits on the throne and from the wrath of the Lamb. The great day of vengeance has come. Who can withstand it?"

All right, the victory in history of the Lamb is about to be proclaimed. Just as the victory of Christians over Jerusalem that rejected the Messiah came about with the fall of Jerusalem in the year seventy A.D., the people of the next persecuted generation are told that the victory is soon to come over Rome itself, over all the onslaught of the Roman Empire. The Lamb has at his disposal all kinds of weapons including death, war, famine, armies of the various nations, to control and put an end to the Roman persecution against them.

Now a halt in the proceedings takes place with chapter 7. "After this I saw four angels standing at the four corners of the earth; they held in check the earth's four winds so that no wind blew on land or sea or through any tree. I saw another angel come up from the east holding the seal of the living God. He cried out at the top of his voice to the four angels who were given power to ravage the land and sea, 'Do no harm to the land or the sea or the trees until we imprint this seal on the foreheads of the servants of our God.'"

This means, "give us time to gather together those who will believe in the Lamb. Give us time to baptize, to bring men into the Christian Church and enpower many Christians throughout the world who will bear the name of God. They'll belong to the family of God. A name meant a great deal to the ancient Israelites. If you bore the name of God you had His seal on your forehead. You were His son. You belonged to Him. You were baptized. You had His life within you. Wait until we make a gathering of God's people throughout the world."

The picture here continues: "I heard the number of those who were so marked with the name of God, one hundred and forty-four thousand from every tribe of Israel. Twelve thousand from the tribe of Judah, twelve thousand from the tribe of Reuben, etc."

Again, we are dealing with the symbolism of numbers. Let's pause and examine them further. First of all, we are not going to take them literally. We need to know something of the ancient literature that interpreted numbers symbolically. Instead of saying "huge crowds" they would give numbers. Now how is one hundred and forty four thousand arrived at? Well, there were twelve tribes of Israel, twelve times twelve is one hundred and forty four. One thousand, to an ancient person, meant a huge multitude. So when one hundred and forty-four is multiplied by one thousand a huge crowd is the result.

To take that literally, as some religionists do, and try to make just 144,000 places in the Heaven of Heavens is to do violence to the text and the meaning here.

"After this I saw before me a huge crowd which no one could count from every nation and race, people and tongue (the Gentiles). They stood before the throne and the Lamb, dressed in long white robes and holding palm branches in their hands." These are the signs and symbols of victory. "They cried out in a loud voice, 'Salvation is from our God who is seated on the throne, and from the Lamb!' All the angels. .. . .said: 'Amen!'"

Then one of the elders asked me, 'Who are these people all dressed in white? And where have they come from? I said to him, 'Sir, you should know better than I.' He then told me, and here's the key to the whole meaning of the book, '"These are the ones who have survived the great period of trial."' There's the perfect definition for the background of apocalyptic literature. These are those who have survived the great period of trial. They have been tested and found worthy of the Lord. '"They have washed their robes and made them white in the blood of the Lamb."' It was this that brought them before God's throne.

"Never again shall they know hunger or thirst. . . the Lamb on the throne will shepherd them." Here is a picture of the Good Shepherd leading His people to green pastures and cool waters.

Now we turn to chapter 8 and the seventh seal. "When the Lamb broke open the seventh seal." We are going to be dealing at length with this seventh seal. It has fascinated many writers, artists and musicians through the centuries. Ingmar Bergman made a film called, "The Seventh Seal". "When the Lamb broke open the seventh seal, there was silence in Heaven for about half an hour." That simply means there was much awe. There was a hush. Something great was about to happen, the final victory.

"Then, as I watched, the seven angels who minister in God's presence were given seven trumpets." The seventh seal is going to be drawn out with seven trumpets, seven bowls of wrath, seven last plagues. Seven and seven and seven because we are dealing with a considerable period of time — much persecution for a century or two here.

"Another angel came in holding a censer of gold. He took his place at the altar of incense and was given large amounts of incense to deposit on the altar of gold in front of the throne, together with the prayers of all God's holy ones." These are the suffering people on earth. Their prayers are coming up before the throne and they're being deposited on the altar by the angels. These prayers have great effect. "From the angel's hand the smoke of the incense went up before God, and with it the prayers of God's people.

"Then the angel took the censer, filled it with live coals from the altar and hurled it down to the earth. Peals of thunder and flashes of lightning followed, and the earth trembled." But notice that just as the Lamb undid the seal and these things happened, people on earth who are suffering are praying, the angels and saints in Heaven are praying, and from that joint prayer incense and coals are put on the censer, and the altar, and finally taken from the altar and thrown on the earth. Now when these coals are thrown on the earth, things happen and they happen as a direct result of the prayers of the suffering people! That's what the author intended to illustrate here. All happens as a direct result of the Lamb's action and of the prayers of the saints.

"The seven angels with the seven trumpets made ready to blow them. When the first angel blew his trumpet, there came hail and then fire mixed with blood, which was hurled down to the earth. A third of the land was scorched . . .

"When the second Angel blew his trumpet, something like a huge mountain all in flames was cast into the sea. A third of the sea turned to blood, a third of the creatures living in the sea died, and a third of the ships were wrecked.

"When the third angel blew his trumpet, a huge star burning like a torch crashed down from the sky. It fell on a third of the rivers and the springs. The stars name was 'Wormwood' because a third part of all the water turned to wormwood. Many people died from the polluted water.

"When the fourth Angel blew his trumpet, a third of the sun, a third of the moon, and a third of the stars were hit hard enough to be plunged into darkness. The day lost a third of its light as did the night."

Now what does all this mean? Don't take it as the end of the world, as we mentioned earlier. All these signs are merely taken from the traditional apocalyptic arsenal of the Old Testament. One may recall here a definite similarity to the plagues of Egypt in the hail and the waters of the River Nile being turned to blood. All of these weapons that God used in Egypt to rescue Israel from Pharaoh are now being used again to save

Christians from Romans. That's all that this means. From the apocalyptic arsenal, from the stage props of the plagues in Egypt, all of these things are being drawn out. And don't take too literally one-third of the Earth being destroyed, one-third of the sea. This is again a literary device used to indicate the extent of God's victory.

"Then the fifth angel blew his trumpet, and I saw a star fall from the sky to the earth. The star was given the key to the shaft of the abyss, he opened it and smoke poured out of the shaft like smoke from an enormous furnace." Literally this is the bottomless pit being opened up, or as we say, all hell breaking loose. Literally the pit of hell is opened up and out of it comes all of the agents of Satan, the enemy of God. "The sun and the air were darkened by the smoke from the shaft. Out of the smoke, onto the land, came locusts . . ." Again the author is drawing from the Egyptian plagues.

These locusts are strange, however. "The pain they inflicted was like that of a scorpion's sting." This is all very symbolic. The locusts were commanded, "to do no harm to the grass in the land or to any plant or tree but only to those men who had not the seal of God on their foreheads." That is, those who are not followers of Jesus. The locusts were not allowed to kill but only "to torture them for five months." That means just a short span of time. The pain they inflicted was like that of a scorpion's sting; so painful, though, that during that time men would seek death but not find it.

"In appearance the locusts were like horses equipped for battle." That means they were strong. The enemy is going to be a strong enemy, "horses equipped for battle." "On their heads they wore something like gold crowns." That means they were going to be given power by God to win some kind of victory for Him or at least to do His will. They had royal authority. "Their faces were like men's faces. But they had hair like women's hair." What this means is that they had apparent strength but weakness, too. "Their teeth were like the teeth of lions, their chests like iron breast plates. Their wings made a sound like the roar of many chariots and horses charging into battle. They had tails with stingers like scorpions. Acting as their king was the angel in charge of the abyss, whose name in Hebrew is Abaddoh and in Greek, Apollyon, (meaning the angel of destruction, another name for the ruler of this bottomless pit).

God gives him power through these mysterious minions of His, described as locusts with all kinds of features that we musn't try to picture. If they were going to win victory and do some of God's work on earth, they had to be given some part of God's royal authority. God is also in charge of Satan's activities. "Satan does nothing without the Lamb letting him." He had to take the lid off the pit before Satan could come out. So the Lamb is in complete charge of history. The saints on earth are given this assurance so that they will know the victory is theirs! They would have merely to endure and be patient for a while in the midst of their trial and testing until the complete victory of the Lamb would come. They might even have to be martyred as Jesus was on Calvary but the victory was theirs. Resurrection was theirs.

The sixth trumpet. "The first woe is past but beware. Then the sixth angel blew his trumpet, and I heard a voice coming from between the horns of the altar of gold in God's presence. It said to the sixth angel who was still holding his trumpet, 'Release the four angels who are tied up on the banks of the great river Euphrates!' So the four angels were released . . . their cavalry troops were two hundred million in number." A numerical exaggeration is made again.

"Now, in my vision, this is how I saw the horses

and their riders. The breast plates they wore were fiery red, deep blue, and pale yellow. The horses' heads were like heads of lions, (i. e., terribly strong) and out of their mouths came fire and sulphur and smoke. By these three plagues— the smoke and sulphur and fire which shot out of their mouths — a third of mankind was slain."

This is a reference to the Parthian armies coming from the East that were to upset and eventually overrun the Roman Empire and set Christians free to live their lives. Note again that they are an instrument of God, just as the plagues of Egypt were an instrument of God given at Moses' command. Here the instruments of God are given at the command from the Lamb.

Let us continue. I want to highlight certain passages of the Book of Revelation and then you can read the rest yourself.

I will make a brief comment on chapter ten. The angel with the scroll came down with one foot on land and one foot on sea. This symbolizes his power and his might as an agent of God. "I was about to start writing when the seven thunders spoke, but I heard a voice from heaven say, 'Seal up what the seven thunders have spoken and do not write it down!'" Seven thunders is merely a euphemistic way of saying God's powerful voice.

The thunders were about to speak in this fashion: "There shall be no more delay. When the time comes for the seventh angel to blow his trumpet, the mysterious plan of God, which he announced to his servants the prophets, shall be accomplished in full." God is completely in command. The mysterious plan of God in history will be accomplished detail for detail.

"Then the voice which I heard from heaven spoke to me again and said, 'Go take the open scroll from the hand of the angel standing on the sea and on the land.' I went up to the angel and said to him, 'Give me the little scroll.' He said to me, 'Here, take it and eat it! It will be sour in your stomach, but in your mouth it will taste as sweet as honey.' I took the little scroll from the angel's hand and ate it. In my mouth it tasted as sweet as honey, but when I swallowed it my stomach turned sour. Then someone said to me, 'You must prophesy again for many peoples and nations, languages and kings.'" If you are familiar with the Book of Ezekiel, you will recognize that the same thing happened to Ezekiel in chapters three and thirty-three. Thus the prophet John is given the same kind of mission that the father of apocalyptic literature, Ezekiel, was given.

"The two witnesses" is a very interesting section. "Someone gave me a measuring rod and said: 'Come and take the measurements of God's temple and altar, and count those who worship there. Exclude the outer court of the temple, however; do not measure it, for it has been handed over to the Gentiles, who will crush the holy city for forty-two months.'"

These are references, once more, to Ezekiel 40 and Zachariah 2, apocalyptic passages that discuss God measuring the temple and the outer court, meaning that God is in charge of every detail. He planned and executed it. The same thing is true here.

"Exclude the outer court of the Temple." That is where the Gentiles, the pagans, lived. When God is measuring the temple, it means he is going to protect the Christians but the outer court, the Roman Empire, is not going to be protected. It has been handed over to the Gentiles who will crush the holy city for forty-two months. What does this mean? Well, as we noted earlier, forty-two months is taken from the apocalyptic arsenal, from the three and one half years of classic persecution during the reign of Antiochus IV, who took Jerusalem in 175 B.C. and committed the abomination of desolation by putting the statue of Zeus in the temple. This terrible period became an archetypal period of persecution for Israel and for Christianity; the forty-two months, or three and a half years or one thousand two hundred and sixty days represent a peak period of persecution that's about to happen for the Christians. The Lord is saying: "Hold tight, endure through it; the victory is yours even though you may have a peak period of suffering as at the time of the abomination of desolation in 175 B.C."

"I will commission my two witnesses to prophesy for those one thousand two hundred and sixty days, dressed in sackcloth." Sackcloth means a time of penance, a time of real prayer and fasting.

Who are these two witnesses? They are Peter and Paul who were persecuted and put to death in 68 B.C. A.D. by the Emperor Nero who, as we shall see presently, is going to be the beast. The Roman Empire is the beast but especially Nero. The two prophets, Peter and Paul, historically were put to death in the same year of the peak of Roman persecution against the Church. That's why we have the forty-two month period. "These are the two olive trees and the two lampstands which stand in the presence of the Lord of the earth." These are references to the Book of Zachariah where mention is made of Joshua and Zerubbabel, the two lampstands, and two witnesses of that time who were God's agents in rebuilding the temple and Israel. The two are now Peter and Paul, not Joshua and Zerubbabel. They are endowed with the same characteristics however. They are lampstands, standing in the presence of the Lord.

"If anyone tries to harm them, fire will come out of the mouths of these witnesses to devour their enemies. Anyone attempting to harm them will surely be slain in this way. These witnesses have power to close up the sky so that no rain will fall during the time of their mission. They also have power to turn water into blood and to afflict the earth at will with any kind of plague."

These are references to the powers given to Christ's Apostles. Jesus said: "You will do even greater things than I have done." (John 12: 14) These powers are described in terms of the powers that Elijah and Moses had. Elijah was able to open and shut the skies, to invoke famine and undo it by his prayer. Moses was able to call down plagues. Peter and Paul had the same power in the New Testament; they had the same authority to set up a new kingdom that Joshua and Zerubbabel had at the time of the reconstruction.

"When they have finished giving their testimony, the wild beast that comes up from the abyss will wage war against them and conquer and kill them." At the time this was written Peter and Paul were dead. The Book of Revelation spans the period between 81 and 90 A.D., most likely, and Peter and Paul were killed in 68 A.D. In apocalyptic literature, however, it is seen as present. "Their corpses will lie in the streets of the great city, which has the symbolic name 'Sodom' or 'Egypt,' where also their Lord was crucified." You know you're dealing with real symbolism now with all of these terms. The city they are going to be killed in is called Sodom, city of paganism, or Egypt, enemy city where their Lord was crucified. Jesus was crucified in Jerusalem which had become Sodom and Gomorrah. As Isaiah said Jerusalem is now Sodom and Gomorrah.

All the cities are merged into one archetypal city of enmity. "Men from every people and race, language and nation, stare at their corpses for three and a half days, a short, symbolic period of time. " . . . but they refuse to bury them. The earth's inhabitants gloat over them and in their merriment exchange gifts, because these two prophets harassed everyone on earth. But after the three and a half days, the breath of life which comes from God returned to them. When they stood on their feet sheer terror gripped those who saw them. The two prophets heard a loud voice from heaven say to them, 'Come up here!' So they went up to heaven in a cloud (as did Jesus, in triumph, or Elijah) as their enemies looked on. At that moment there was a violent earthquake and a tenth of the city fell in ruins." They are going to be vindicated, that's what this means. The martyrs will be vindicated and the chief martyrs will certainly be vindicated.

"Then the seventh angel blew his trumpet. Loud voices in heaven cried out," and here's the key phrase, I think, of the whole Book of Revelation, "The kingdom of the world now belongs to our Lord and to his Anointed One, and he shall reign forever and ever." Or you will see the Son of Man coming on the clouds with power and majesty, and Jesus will be Lord. The kingdom of the world will belong to Jesus and he will be victor, ultimate victor, Lord of the world and of heaven. This promise is given to the faithful martyrs and then a hymn of praise is sung.

6 The Woman and the Dragon

We turn now to chapter twelve, the famous chapter of "the Woman and the Dragon." What does this mean? It may be a little difficult to understand.

"A great sign appeared in the sky, a woman clothed with the sun, with the moon under her feet, and on her head a crown of twelve stars." This is a reference, typical in the Old Testament, concerning Israel as Mother Zion, virgin Zion, daughter Zion. Israel, the whole nation, is pictured as a woman giving birth to sons of God.

The Israelite nation is the main focus here. It is often seen, however, as the Virgin Mary. This is not, done wrongfully either because she incarnated the Israelite nation when she gave birth to the Messiah. The Israelite nation is pictured ordinarily as giving birth to the Messiah, and of course it was through the woman Mary that the Messiah came.

So the great sign is this woman clothed with the sun, given cosmic proportions now because the Lord is with her. "The moon under her feet, and on her head a crown of twelve stars. Because she was with child, (Jesus) she wailed aloud in pain (pains of childbirth, Messianic pains of birth in times of crisis) as she labored to give birth.

Then another sign appeared in the sky: it was a huge dragon, flaming red, with seven heads and ten horns." This is Satan, the dragon, doing battle with God. The huge dragon has cosmic proportions also, it's tail sweeping one-third of the stars out of the way.

It is a huge enemy. Paul says our battle is "not against flesh and blood but against principalities, princes and powers." *(Eph 6: 10)*

And a lot of power. Seven heads and ten horns. Notice, however, that it is lopsided, unlike the seven horns and eyes indicating the perfection of God. "The dragon stood before the woman about to give birth, ready to devour her child when it should be born. She gave birth to a son — a boy destined to shepherd all the nations with an iron rod (Jesus). Her child was caught up to God and to his throne." Here we have a reference to the Ascension.

Notice that Satan wants to devour the child; he did figuratively speaking, when Jesus was crucified on Calvary. He said: "This is the hour of Satan", applying His death to the work of Satan. Satan entered Judas and succeeded in having Jesus captured. Satan, in a sense, had a temporary victory, a seeming victory over the Messiah. The dragon was trying to prevent the reign of God. However, it was only an illusory victory because the child was caught up to God and to his throne.

And the woman, the Israelite nation, the new Israel, the Church herself, now fled into the desert, the typical place of refuge from the enemy, "Where a special place had been prepared for her by God; there she was taken care of for one thousand two hundred and sixty days". This again is the typical three and a half years of terrible persecution.

Then war broke out in heaven; Michael and his angels battled against the dragon. Although the dragon and his angels fought back, they were overpowered and lost their place in heaven. The huge dragon, the ancient serpent known as the devil or Satan, the seducer of the whole world, was driven out; he was hurled down to earth and his minions with him.

"Then I heard a loud voice in heaven say, 'now have salvation and power come, the reign of our God and the authority of his Anointed One. For the accuser of our brothers is cast out."

When the dragon saw that he had been cast down to the earth, he pursued the woman. Just as he pursued Jesus, he now is pursuing the Church, individual Christians. "But the woman was given the wings of a gigantic eagle so that she could fly off to her place in the desert." God promised protection to the Church; the jaws of Hell would not come against it. "Where, far from the serpent, she could be taken care of for a year and for two and a half years more. The three and a half year period is employed again.

"The serpent, however, spewed a torrent of water out of his mouth to search out the woman and sweep her away. The earth then came to the woman's rescue by opening its mouth and swallowing the flood which the dragon spewed out of his mouth.

"Enraged at her escape, the dragon went off to make war on the rest of her offspring, on those who kept God's commandments and give witness to Jesus. He took up his position by the shore of the sea." We have now the standing combat between Satan and Christians transferred from Jesus to the Body of Christ.

7   The Two Beasts

"Then I saw a wild beast come out of the sea with
ten horns and seven heads; on its horns were ten
diadems and on its heads blasphemous names."
(Chapter 13)

Note this, the beast here is in the service of the
dragon. The dragon had just engaged in a war against
Christ and the Church. And now out of the sea, at the
service of the dragon, a beast appears with ten horns
and seven heads. This is the Roman Empire with its
satellite kings working with it's governors and other
officials.

A long standing tradition depicts the beast dwelling
in the sea, from the primeval chaos of the waters in
Genesis, through the history of art the beast is often
seen as coming out of the sea. The movie *Jaws* is
probably a remnant of that tradition. The sea is a
symbol of the enemy of God, the enemy of God's
people. It is a shifty place often pictured as the lair of
death because of its uncertainty and its death traps. It
is the lair of Satan.

"The dragon gave it his own power and throne,
together with great authority. I noticed that one of the
beast's heads seemed to have been mortally wounded, but this mortal wound was healed. In wonder-
ment, the whole world followed after the beast." This
is a reference to a legend that Nero, who had killed
himself with a self-inflicted wound, was going to
come back to life again. This is the allusion in the
references to a mortally wounded beast. Actually in

one of his descendants Domitian, Nero did live again with an even greater ferociousness. I think that's the reference here.

"Men worshipped the dragon for giving his authority to the beast; they also worshipped the beast." This is emperor worship. "The beast was given a mouth for uttering proud boasts and blasphemies, but the authority it received was to last only forty-two months." That's all God would allow. "It began to hurl blasphemies against God, reviling him and the members of his heavenly household as well. The beast was allowed (note that the beast was *allowed* by God who was in command) "to wage war against God's people and conquer them." This is similar to the allowance of Jesus' death. "It was likewise granted authority over every race and people, language and nation. The beast will be worshipped by all those inhabitants of earth who did not have their names written at the world's beginning in the book of the living, which belongs to the Lamb who was slain."

"Such is the faithful endurance that distinguishes God's holy people." Again we have the theme of the book: the call for endurance until the victory is won in the battle between God and Satan.

The second beast. There are two beasts in the service of the dragon. The first was the political beast, Nero and his followers, of whom Domitian was the worst. "Then I saw another wild beast come up out of the earth; it had two horns (a little beast) like a ram and it spoke like a dragon." The big booming voice denotes the power of the dragon. It used the authority of the first beast, the emperor, to promote its interests by making the world and all its inhabitants worship the first beast whose mortal wound had been healed. This is a reference to the priests of Rome who led the people in emperor worship, who made the people worship the emperor or die. This beast performed great prodigies. It could even make fire come down from heaven to earth as men looked on. It is just like the magicians under Pharaoh in the Old Testament.

"Because of the prodigies it was allowed to perform by authority of the first beast, it led astray the earth's inhabitants, telling them to make an idol in honor of the beast that had been wounded by the sword and yet lived." This is a reference to statues of Nero that spoke. "The second wild beast was then permitted to give life to the beast's image, so that the image had the power of speech and of putting to death anyone who refused to worship it." This is a reference to Satanic tricks, to the worship in these temples, to oracles speaking, and prodigies happening, all of which seduced people. Satan can work signs and wonders as Jesus warned in the apocalypses of Matthew, Mark and Luke: " . . . Beware of false messiahs who will work signs and wonders so as to deceive the elect if that were possible." *(Mt. 24:24)*

It's a fact that in first-century Rome there were all kinds of prodigies, just as it's a fact that Egyptian magicians worked prodigies almost as powerful as those of Moses. This is the power of Satan. Satan today has that same kind of power. One reads literature about the astounding manifestations of Satanic power in the occult world. Sometimes, in the name of Christianity, angels of light have this power. But because of the misuse of this power, Jesus warned against false messiahs working signs and wonders to the deception of the elect. There are false apparitions, so-called apparitions of Christ or Mary today. Just in the last few years I've heard of apparitions of Mary, accompanied by signs and wonders for example, in several states, all of which I'm sure are not true. But seeming signs and wonders accompany this to deceive the elect if that were possible.

The same kind of things are happening today with worship of false Messiahs. All kinds of esoteric religions have sprung up accompanied by signs and wonders geared to deceive the elect. The Book of Revelation warns against this very sort of thing.

So much for the second beast in the service of the first beast, emperor worship, working signs and wonders and deceiving a lot of people. This is the power of the dragon. This is the battle that was going on. "It forced all men, small and great, rich and poor, slave and free, to accept a stamped image on their right hand or their forehead," in other words to have the name of the beast. One either belonged to God or one belonged to the beast.

This apocalyptic literature is very straightforward. One is either on God's side or on Satan's. One bore the name of God, and was branded with the mark of God, or one bore the name of Satan and was branded with the mark of Satan. "It did not allow a man to buy or sell anything unless he was first marked with the name of the beast." Christians could not live in Rome unless they worshipped the beast. That's why many of them were martyred.

A certain wisdom is needed here with regard to the coded message of the apocalypse. With a little ingenuity anyone can calculate the number of the beast for it is the number of a certain man. The man's number is 666. In coded message this meant Caesar-Nero, or the Roman Emperor. In Hebrew language each letter of the alphabet was given a symbolic, numerical value and if one adds in Hebrew letters, the letters of Caesar-Nero, one will have six hundred and sixty-six.

Down through history this figure has been misinterpreted as Hitler, Mussolini and many others.

Chapter fourteen I won't go into. It's just a song about the Victory of the Lamb and the companions of the Lamb, the huge crowd of Christian martyrs who share in His victory.

8 "Babylon is Fallen"

ch.14

An angel finally cries out, "Fallen, fallen is Babylon the great . . . she has made all the nations drink the poisoned wine of her lewdness". The text then tells of kings committing fornication with Babylon the great, the great harlot, who with her prostitution led astray the whole world, just as Jezebel had done. This is not, contrary to what one may think, a reference to sexual immorality. In biblical imagery it means unfaithfulness to the one true God, or adultery, and worship of other gods. It is like a woman who deserts her husband, and in adultery or fornication, consorts with other men. It simply means idolatry, those who like Jezebel would lead God's followers to an adulterous union with other gods or into emperor worship.

But the cry came out: "Hold on! Babylon is about to fall." "Babylon" is a symbolic name here for Rome. It's coded to protect the Christians who might be found with this book. "There shall be no relief day or night for those who worship the beast or its image or accept the mark of its name. This is what sustains the holy ones, who keep the commandments of God and have faith in Jesus.

"I heard a voice from heaven say to me: 'Write this down: Happy now are the dead who die in the Lord!' The Spirit added, 'Yes, they shall find rest from their labors, for their good works accompany them.'

"Then, as I watched, a white cloud appeared and on the cloud sat One like a Son of Man wearing a gold crown on his head and holding a sharp sickle in his hand.' Jesus as the Son of Man in Daniel is coming on the clouds holding a sharp sickle in His hand ready to reap the harvest of earth. The meaning is quite evident.

There is an interesting line in verse 20, "The wine-press was trodden." All the grapes are out by the sickle. The harvest is cut and the winepress was trodden (note the significant little phrase) "Outside the city." Recall that Jesus was crucified outside the city. This is a veiled reference to the Blood of the Lamb, shed outside the city. It is a parallel to the blood of the martyrs shed outside the city. One Blood in one Body redeeming the world.

The seven last plagues are self explanatory. There is almost a repetition of earlier passages with the plagues of Egypt again brought forth to be used by the Lamb in conquering the beast and winning the victory for the Christians. The same kinds of things happen as in earlier chapters: armies, death, famine, coming again as we get ready for the final victory of the Lamb.

Let us examine chapter 16, verse 17. "Finally, the seventh angel poured out his bowl upon the empty air. From the throne in the sanctuary came a loud voice which said, 'It is finished!' There followed lightning flashes and peals of thunder, then a violent earthquake. Such was its violence that there has never been one like it in all the time men have lived on the earth. The great city was split into three parts, and the other Gentile cities also fell. God remembered Babylon, the great, giving her the cup filled with the blazing wine of his wrath. Every island fled and mountains disappeared. Giant hailstones like huge weights came crashing down on mankind from the sky, and men blasphemed God for the plague of hailstones, because this plague was so severe." Again, apocalyptic imagery from the arsenal is used to describe more plagues that would eventually overcome Rome and prepare for the emergence of a new world.

"Then one of the seven angels . . . said, 'Come, I will show you the judgement in store for the great harlot who sits by the waters of the deep. The kings of the earth have committed fornication with her, and the earth's inhabitants have grown drunk on the wine of her lewdness . . . I saw a woman seated on a scarlet beast which was covered with blasphemous names."

This is right out of Zechariah where one has the scarlet women and the basket, a symbol of wickedness who, incidentally, was transported to Babylon. "On her forehead was written a symbolic name" (notice the symbolic name) "Babylon, the great, mother of harlots and all the world's abominations. I saw that the woman was drunk with the blood of God's holy ones and the blood of those martyred for their faith in Jesus". This is a symbolic picturing of the Roman Empire described as the woman of wickedness.

In a subsequent part of the chapter is described the meaning of the beast and the harlot. The author very clearly states in verse 7, "I will explain to you the symbolism of the woman and of the seven-headed and ten-horned beast carrying her. The beast you saw existed once, and now exists no longer. It will come up from the abyss once more." That's the reference to the legend of Nero dying and coming back to life again, as he himself predicted. But it is in one of his sons, Domitian. "It will come up from the abyss once more before going to final ruin. All of the men of the earth whose names have not been written in the book of the living . . . shall be amazed when they see the beast, for it existed once and now exists no longer, and yet it will exist again."

Here is the clue, for one who possesses discernment. "The seven heads are seven hills on which the woman sits enthroned". The seven-hilled city, although it is not named, is the empire of Rome.

"They are also seven kings: five have already fallen, one lives now, and the last has not yet come." The book can be dated from this sentence. Five of the persecuting Roman Emperors are dead. It says one is living now and one is yet to come. But when he does come he will remain only a short while.

"The ten horns you saw represent ten satellite kings who have not yet been crowned; they will possess royal authority along with the beast, but only for an hour. Then they will come to agreement and bestow their power and authority on the beast. They will fight against the Lamb but the Lamb will conquer them, for he is the Lord of lords and the King of kings; victorious, too, will be his followers — the ones who are called: the chosen and the faithful."

And then in chapter 18 there is a long dirge on the fall of Babylon, or Rome. It is very much like Ezekiel 28 on the fall of Tyre, that proud city. Again note the appeal to the father of apocalyptic literature, Ezekiel.

9   Victory of the Lamb

Chapter 19 is a beautiful chapter on the Lord of Lords and King of Kings, the Word of God, Jesus Christ. He is described as the Gospels describe him, the Bridegroom coming to wed his Church in the beautiful wedding feast. Christians are described as the bride of the Lamb invited to the wedding feast.

"(The linen dress is the virtuous deeds of God's saints.)"..Happy are they who have been invited to the wedding feast of the Lamb." He is pictured as destroying the beast and getting rid of all the enemies of God. He is riding on a white horse, "His eyes blazed like fire, and on his head are many diadems. Inscribed on his person was a name known to no one but himself." He is unique. "He wore a cloak that had been dipped in blood." (The blood of Calvary.) "And His name was the Word of God. The armies of heaven were behind him riding white horses and dressed in fine linen, pure and white. Out of his mouth came a sharp sword" (the word of God as Hebrews 4 says, a two-edged sword) "for striking down the nations. He will shepherd them with an iron rod; it is he who will tread out in the winepress the blazing wrath of God the Almighty'" King of Kings and Lord of Lords."

I said earlier that ninety-five per cent of the Book of Revelation is over and done with at the end of the first century. There is a short section towards the end of the book, however, that talks about the future history of the world and the ultimate victory of the Lord.

First, in chapter 20, there's a reference to "the

thousand year reign." This must not be taken literally, because it really means just a long period of time. Those who try to pin it down with a millenarian have always failed. Symbolically, it simply means a long period of time. And it refers to the Church upon earth, a long period of time where Christ, and the faithful Christians, and those martyred with Christ would reign on earth. And then it discusses, a little later, when the thousand years are over, of the end of the world's history. I would take this to be a sort of new unleashing of Satan. Released from his prison, he goes out to seduce the nations in all corners of the earth and muster people for war. There is a final last battle where the Lamb will slay him and put him in the pit forever, where the second death occurs. Those who have been part of Satan's troops are with him forever in sulphur and brimstone, never-to-be-extinguished-fire, but those who have followed the Lamb will reign with him in the resurrection. They won't have to fear the second death, the eternal judgement, the eternal alienation from God. They will be with the Lamb forever.

The new Jerusalem is then described: "It is coming down from heaven." This is a reference, not just to the eternal kingdom the Lamb will provide, but even the kingdom of the Church on earth. The Church is the Bride of the Lamb, the place where God dwells. It is a kingdom coming down from heaven to earth, a new Jerusalem, a city with twelve gates, representing the twelve Apostles.

It is the Church, a beautiful picture described in rich imagery. There is gold and silver and precious jewels of all sorts. There is no temple in the city because the Lord Jesus is the temple and he's the Lamb and he's the Priest and everything in that temple!

There follows a picture of paradisiacal splendor: rich fruit, the tree of life growing continuously. It's leaves are for the healing of the nations and it blooms each month. The kingdom of the world has become the kingdom of Our God and Our Lord. No wonder that towards the end of the book the Christian cries out along with the Holy Spirit, the Spirit and the Bride. The Holy Spirit and the Church cry, "Come! . . . Come Lord Jesus!" Inaugurate this world. Come in triumph. Come in victory. We want to get into your Kingdom.

And thus the Book of Revelation ends with the cry that characterized the early Christian, "Maranatha, Come, Lord Jesus!" Come in power. Come in judgement. Take over this world. We are tired of living in a world where you are not Lord, where there's persecution for those who follow you. Come and be Lord. Set up Your kingdom even here, Lord. And in response the Lord promises that He will come, and come soon and do it. Endure and the victory will be yours! Alleluia!

CONTEMPLATIVE PRAYER: Problems and An Approach for the Ordinary Christian

Rev. Alan J. Placa $1.75

This inspiring book covers much ground: the struggle of prayer, growth in familiarity with the Lord and the sharing process. In addition, he clearly outlines a method of contemplative prayer for small groups based on the belief that private communion with God is essential to, and must precede, shared prayer. The last chapter provides model prayers, taken from our Western heritage, for the enrichment of private prayer experience.

REASONS FOR REJOICING
Experiences in Christian Hope

Rev. Kenneth J. Zanca

God's love is a gift, not a reward. This realization marks the beginning of mature faith and steeps our lives in confidence and joy. In clear, non-pious, non-technical language, Father Zanca offers a way to interpret the religious dimension in the everyday experiences of being forgiven, seeking God, praying, celebrating and confronting suffering/evil.

"It is a refreshing Christian approach to the Good News, always emphasizing the love and mercy of God in our lives, and our response to that love in Christian hope." Brother Patrick Hart, Secretary to the late Thomas Merton

THE ONE WHO LISTENS: A Book of Prayer 2.25

By Rev. Michael Hollings and Etta Gullick. Here the Spirit speaks through men and women of the past (St. John of the Cross, Thomas More, Dietrich Bonhoeffer), and present (Michael Quoist, Mother Teresa, Malcolm Boyd). There are also prayers from men of other faiths such as Muhammed and Tagore. God meets us where we are and since men share in sorrow, joy and anxiety, *their* prayers are *our* prayers. This is a book that will be outworn, perhaps, but never outgrown.

ENFOLDED BY CHRIST: An Encouragement to Pray 1.95

By Rev. Michael Hollings. This book helps us toward giving our lives to God in prayer yet at the same time remaining totally available to our fellowman — a difficult but possible feat. Father's sharing of his own difficulties and his personal approach convince us that "if he can do it, we can." We find in the author a true spiritual guardian and friend.

**Order from your bookstore or
LIVING FLAME PRESS, Locust Valley, N.Y. 11560**

PETALS OF PRAYER: Creative Ways To Pray

By Rev. Paul Sauvé   1.50

"*Petals of Prayer is an extremely practical book for anyone who
desires to pray but has difficulty finding a method for so doing. At
least 15 different methods of prayer are described and illustrated in
simple, straightforward ways, showing they can be contemporary
even though many of them enjoy a tradition of hundreds of years.
In an excellent introductory chapter, Fr. Sauvé states that the best
'method' of prayer is the one which unites us to God. . . . Father
Sauvé masterfully shows how traditional methods of prayer can be
very much in tune with a renewed church.*"
St. Anthony Messenger

CRISIS OF FAITH
Invitation to Christian Maturity   1.50

By Rev. Thomas Keating, ocso. How to hear ourselves called to
discipleship in the Gospels is Abbot Thomas' important and engrossing message. As Our Lord forms His disciples, and deals with His
friends or with those who come asking for help in the Gospels, we
can receive insights into the way He is forming or dealing with us in
our day to day lives.

IN GOD'S
PROVIDENCE:
The Birth of a Catholic
Charismatic Parish

1.25

By Rev. John Randall. The engrossing story of the now well-known
Word of God Prayer Community in St. Patrick's Parish, Providence,
R.I. as it developed from Father Randall's first adverse reaction to
the budding Charismatic Movement to today as it copes with the
problems of being a truly pioneer Catholic Charismatic Parish.

"*This splendid little volume bubbles over with joy and peace, with
'Spirit' and work.*"
The Priest

Order from your bookstore or
LIVING FLAME PRESS, Locust Valley, N.Y. 11560

SEEKING PURITY OF HEART:
THE GIFT OF OURSELVES TO GOD

illus **1.25**

By Joseph Breault. For those of us who feel that we do not live up
to God's calling, that we have sin of whatever shade within our
hearts. This book shows how we can begin a journey which will lead
from our personal darkness to wholeness in Christ's light — a purity
of heart. Clear, practical help is given us in the constant struggle to
free ourselves from the deceptions that sin has planted along all
avenues of our lives.

PROMPTED BY THE SPIRIT

2.25

By Rev. Paul Sauvé. A handbook by a Catholic Charismatic Renewal
national leader for all seriously concerned about the future of the
renewal and interested in finding answers to some of the problems
that have surfaced in small or large prayer groups. It is a call to all
Christians to find answers with the help of a wise Church tradition
as transmitted by her ordained ministers. The author has also
written *Petals of Prayer/Creative Ways to Pray.*

DISCOVERING PATHWAYS TO PRAYER

1.75

By Msgr. David E. Rosage. Following Jesus was never meant to be
dull, or worse, just duty-filled. Those who would aspire to a life of
prayer and those who have already begun, will find this book amaz-
ingly thorough in its scripture-punctuated approach.

*"A simple but profound book which explains the many ways and
forms of prayer by which the person hungering for closer union
with God may find him."* **Emmanuel Spillane, O.C.S.O., Abbott,
Our Lady of the Holy Trinity Abbey, Huntsville, Utah.**

Order from your bookstore or
LIVING FLAME PRESS, Locust Valley, N.Y. 11560

Books by Venard Polusney, O. Carm.

UNION WITH THE LORD IN PRAYER
Beyond Meditation To Affective Prayer Aspiration And Contemplation
.85

"A magnificent piece of work. It touches on all the essential points of Contemplative Prayer. Yet it brings such a sublime subject down to the level of comprehension of the 'man in the street,' and in such an encouraging way."
Abbott James Fox, O.C.S.O. (former superior of Thomas Merton at the Abbey of Gethsemani)

ATTAINING SPIRITUAL MATURITY FOR CONTEMPLATION (According to St. John of the Cross)
.85

"I heartily recommend this work with great joy that at last the sublime teachings of St. John of the Cross have been brought down to the understanding of the ordinary Christian without at the same time watering them down. For all (particularly for charismatic Christians) hungry for greater contemplation."
Rev. George A Maloney, S.J., Editor of Diakonia, Professor of Patristics and Spirituality, Fordham University.

THE PRAYER OF LOVE ... THE ART OF ASPIRATION
1.50

"It is the best book I have read which evokes the simple and loving response to remain in love with the Lover. To read it meditatively, to imbibe its message of love, is to have it touch your life and become part of what you are."
Mother Dorothy Guilbault, O. Carm., Superior General, Lacombe, La.

From the writings of John of St. Samson, O. Carm., mystic and charismatic

PRAYER, ASPIRATION AND CONTEMPLATION
Translated and edited by Venard Poslusney, O. Carm. Paper 3.95

All who seek help in the exciting journey toward contemplation will find in these writings of John of St. Samson a compelling inspiration and support along with the practical guidance needed by those who travel the road of prayer.

**Order from your bookstore or
LIVING FLAME PRESS, Locust Valley, N.Y. 11560**

LIVING FLAME PRESS
BOX 74
LOCUST VALLEY, N.Y. 11560

Order from your bookstore or use this coupon.

Please send me:

Quantity
_____ **The Book of Revelation—$1.75**
_____ **Reasons for Rejoicing — $1.75**
_____ **Discovering Pathways to Prayer — $1.75**
_____ **Prompted by the Spirit — $2.25**
_____ **Prayer of Love — $1.50**
_____ **Prayer, Aspiration & Contemplation — $3.95**
_____ **Union with the Lord — $.85**
_____ **Enfolded by Christ — $1.95**
_____ **Contemplative Prayer — $1.75**
_____ **Attaining Spiritual Maturity — $.85**
_____ **Petals of Prayer — $1.50**
_____ **Seeking Purity of Heart — $1.25**
_____ **Crisis of Faith — $1.50**
_____ **In God's Providence — $1.25**
_____ **The One Who Listens — $2.25**

QUANTITY ORDER: DISCOUNT RATES
For convents, prayer groups, etc.: $10 to $25 = 10%;
$26 to $50 = 15%; over $50 = 20%.
Booksellers: 40%, 30 days net.

NAME_____

ADDRESS _____

CITY _____STATE _____ ZIP_____
[ ] *Payment enclosed. Kindly include $.35 postage and handling
on order up to $3.00. Above that, include 5% of total. Thank
you.*